P9-DNG-164

FROM THE TOP DOWN

THE EXECUTIVE ROLE IN VOLUNTEER PROGRAM SUCCESS

REVISED EDITION

SUSAN J. ELLIS

With special sections on
legal issues by Jeffrey D. Kahn, Esq.
and accounting questions by Alan S. Glazer, CPA

Library of Congress Cataloging-in-Publication Data

Ellis, Susan J.
    From the top down: the executive role in volunteer pro-
gram success / Susan J. Ellis, Jeffrey D. Kahn, Alan S. Glazer.
— Rev. ed.
        p.   cm.
    Includes bibliographical references and index.
    ISBN 0-940576-17-1 (pbk.)
    1. Voluntarism—Management. 2. Personnel manage-
ment. 3. Volunteers. I. Kahn, Jeffrey D. II. Glazer, Alan S.
III. Title.
HN49. V64E44   1996
361. 3'7'068—dc20   96-22527
                                                          CIP

Copyright © 1996 by Energize, Inc.
                        5450 Wissahickon Avenue
                        Philadelphia, PA 19144

Second printing, 1999.

ISBN 0-940576-17-1

This is a fully-revised edition of the book originally published in
1986 by Energize.

Printed in the USA.

CONTENTS

ACKNOWLEDGEMENTS

No book ever springs full blown from the mind of an author. Rather, it evolves slowly from personal experience, research, innumerable conversations, and active listening to the concerns of others. The participants in my workshops over twenty years will never know how their various questions (and comments about the first edition) sparked ideas that found their way into the following pages—thank you to you all!

I am grateful to the many people who, in one way or another, contributed to the content of this revision. Jeffrey Kahn once again contributed his legal perspective—I always value your keen mind and warm support, Jeff. Alan Glazer provided his up-to-the-minute expertise to assure that this new edition explains the most recent accounting information. Todd Peterson's careful proofreading uncovered fine points overlooked even the first time around—a man after my own detail-oriented heart! Thanks, too, to Kristin Floyd Gillern for her excellent suggestions, to Melanie Etemad for her help with the Index, to Peter Chiarelli and Penny Keller at Kutztown Publishing for their conscientious page layouts, and to Diane Miljat for her great cover design.

Most especially, my sincere appreciation to everyone who bought and read the original edition of *From the Top Down* and then took the time to let me know its value to them. Your encouragement made me determined to keep the book in print and updated. May there come a time when executive attention to the subject of volunteers is so second-nature that this book becomes an historical oddity!

INTRODUCTION

The following—in its entirety—was the introduction to the first edition of this book, written in 1986. Upon revisiting it ten years later, I was struck by the continued relevance of the words I chose so carefully a decade ago. Much has changed in the world and also in volunteerism. But the basic need for this book and rationale for executive involvement in questions relating to volunteers have only become clearer. So please read on...and I'll rejoin you with a revised-edition note at the end of the section.

Most books and articles about volunteer program management are designed for the direct supervisor of volunteers. Such frontline managers are the usual audience in the more than 1500 training workshops Energize, Inc. has conducted across the country since 1977. Our workshops (as well as individualized consultation sessions) deal with all aspects of how to start, maintain, or expand the utilization of volunteers in organizations that range from hospitals to courts to museums to schools. The skills of volunteer administration are generic and apply to all settings. After years of training and consulting with so many leaders of volunteers, I have become convinced that many of their concerns stem directly from a lack of substantive support from their agencies' top administrators. This lack of support is not due to malice or unwillingness to be of help, but is rather due to the failure of executives to understand what is really needed from them.

That is why this book has been written for *top level executives* of agencies that already involve volunteers or that are considering starting a volunteer program. Very little has been published about the volunteer-related issues that deserve executive attention. It is probably an accurate assumption that most exec-

utives were not taught anything about volunteers in their formal
schooling. There may have been some time spent on the interrelationship of executives with their boards of directors, which is
one aspect of working successfully with volunteers, but few management texts or lecturers speak to the specific issues that will be
raised in these pages.

Many volunteer programs suffer from "benign neglect."
Only if and when something goes wrong does the executive
become involved. Too few CEOs monitor the day-to-day progress of the volunteer program or give the director of volunteers
the benefit of ongoing suggestions or input from the administrative perspective. Some executives view volunteers as a "nice"
thing to have—"auxiliary" in all the diminutive connotations of
that word—but not necessarily as something requiring much
management attention.

What a mistake! Perhaps the worst result is that too many
volunteer programs languish from a lack of *expectations*—limited
vision that stops volunteers from achieving their fullest impact or
productivity. The unfortunate fact is that more volunteers are
underutilized than are overburdened.

The target audience of this book is the top decision-maker.
You might be the executive director of a nonprofit agency or its
board president; you might be the CEO of a large institution,
whether profit-making or not; or you might be the director of a
government agency. While some of the issues presented here
may differ for the specifics or size of your particular setting, there
are really more similarities than differences between the types of
organizations that utilize volunteers.

Your organization may have no volunteers at present or
may already benefit from a large, well-established volunteer
corps. It is never too soon nor too late to examine the concerns
outlined in the following pages.

You may be seeking volunteers who are specialists in specific fields or those who are generalists—or both. The types of
assignments your organization offers to volunteers may range
from long-term, ongoing work to one-time special events; some
may need to be done on-site in your facility, while other assignments may involve independent work in the community. You
may call volunteer work by labels such as "community service,"
"citizen participation," "public service," "internships," "communi-

ty involvement," "self-help," or *pro bono publico* work. Regardless of the scope, diversity, or vocabulary of the volunteer program you plan, the basic principles discussed here will apply.

This book is not meant to be a distillation of all the resources available on how to develop and manage a volunteer program. Whomever you designate to direct volunteers is encouraged to seek out those resources and learn more about the details of effective, daily volunteer administration. Rather, this book deals with issues that are directly in your control as the executive. It is also designed to be thought-provoking and provide you with a basis upon which to make necessary decisions.

Some of the concepts proposed in the following pages may seem radical. Actually, there is a fair mix of suggestions based on time-proven principles and of proposals articulated in print for the first time. In order to stimulate and stretch perspectives, however, I present the most logical extension of the way the best volunteer programs operate. You are free, of course, to pick and choose among the recommendations here to develop the form of volunteer administration that will best meet your own organization's needs.

Some readers may be feeling a bit uncomfortable in the suspicion that I am going to suggest a great deal of structure to bureaucratize volunteerism. The fact is that successful volunteering does not come from spontaneous combustion. Most of our organizations today are already rather complex and, unless we develop clear ways for volunteers to participate in our activities, people really do not know how to become involved. This is true whether the organization is an "agency," an "institution," or an all-volunteer association.

It is also important to avoid wasting the time of volunteers—which is exactly what happens if there has been insufficient planning to define and prepare the work to be done. It is a form of volunteer recognition to establish standards for who can become a volunteer, how assignments are made, and whether accomplishments will be evaluated. The best volunteer program management serves to *enable* volunteer achievement, not limit it.

All the management principles that work effectively with employees apply equally to volunteers. But surprisingly enough, the theme of this book is not necessarily to treat volunteers in the same way you would treat salaried staff. Volunteer administration emphasizes motivators such as choice, positive working environment, and recognition, to which all workers will respond with increased morale and productivity. So, this book proposes that it may be better management practice to *treat employees as though they were volunteers!*

The first step to volunteer program success is *vision.* Volunteers can expand the horizons of your organization and your staff. Encourage volunteers to be creative and innovative partners in service delivery, and then expect the best. Self-fulfilling prophecy is a key factor. If your concept of what volunteers can contribute is limited, you will design a volunteer program structure that indeed keeps achievement low. But if you are open to the potential of what might develop, you will find ways to encourage volunteers' success.

The second step is *commitment.* You must have the conviction that volunteers are important...that they are the "non-salaried personnel" of the agency. Volunteers are not "added spice" to your organizational mix. Instead, they are one of the main ingredients. As top executive, you can establish and enforce this premise throughout your organization.

As we will examine in the following chapter, it is important to have a clear understanding of why volunteers are valuable in your setting. Articulating the reasons for involving volunteers is an executive level responsibility...and it forms the foundation on which your organization will build its volunteer participation.

Now, here are a few thoughts from the perspective of the revised edition...

I spent many hours rereading—and reconsidering—the first edition of *From the Top Down*, updating material and adding items to each chapter that have evolved in the past decade. Again, the continuing relevance of most of the material is both comforting and disturbing. Some of the issues about moving from lip service to true support have concerned me since my days as a volunteer program director back in the early 1970s. On the other hand, there has been progress and the outlook for the future is positive.

What have been some of the major changes in the past ten years?

First, the volunteer world has expanded to welcome an ever-growing range of new people seeking service opportunities. As you will see, these folks do not necessarily label themselves as "volunteers," but they are certainly a resource. At the same time, certain traditional types of volunteering are disappearing or metamorphosing into new forms. Depending on which expert's research you prefer, we are either turning our backs on the old "nation of joiners" or we are "rediscovering community." These observations are not necessarily contradictory and both may be true. The question is whether your organization can adapt to the valid needs and wants of volunteers today.

As the definition and use of the word "volunteer" changes, other vocabulary issues have been recognized. For example, it is a valid observation that volunteers are not a "program." Obviously this book will continue to use the common language of "volunteer program" to convey the organized integration of volunteers into an agency's service delivery. But conceptually, we usually use the word "program" for types of services. We do not speak of "the employee program," do we? Employees *provide* programs. So do volunteers.

The reference to "managing" volunteers is also questionable. Some have pointed out that one manages programs, not people. Even more important, however, is that the term "managing" implies that volunteers are always a group of workers to be directed. To get the most out of volunteer involvement (and probably out of employees, too), the best choice is the approach of *leading* volunteers.

Over the last decade, the profession of "volunteer administration" has made rapid strides in the training of leaders of volunteer programs. The number of books on how to work effectively with volunteers has quadrupled. (The resources in Appendix B are almost completely new to this edition.) Volunteerism conferences attract over a thousand at the international/national level and hundreds at the state or provincial level. It is increasingly possible for someone to learn about volunteer program development and management at the local level through regular workshops, some college courses and certificate programs, and professional societies. However, not much progress has been made in the training of administrators and other agency staff for whom volunteer management is not a major responsibility, but who must interface daily with volunteers.

Despite the recommendations in this book about "best practices," it is useful to realize that *there are no rules* when it comes to the successful involvement of volunteers. This is one area in which inventiveness and creativity still apply. While the techniques of the "profession" of volunteer management are important, my goal is certainly not to box community participation into a model designed solely as a parallel to staff operations. Barter, walk-in volunteering, collaboration, self-help, shared volunteers, volunteer exchanges—if it works for you, do it! Understand the *principles* of how to welcome volunteers and the rest will follow.

As we approach the end of the century, of the millennium, we are facing major changes in government priorities and how we pay for the services we want. Whether you are with a not-for-profit agency or a unit of government, you are undoubtedly redesigning your budget and exploring future funding sources. You may be the head of one of the growing number of for-profit companies in human service delivery, but still exploring valid ways to involve volunteers on behalf of clients. The question of whether and how volunteers fit into any organization's "resource mix" is as pertinent as it ever was.

It's not just money, of course. Many organizations, perhaps with health care showing the way, are going to be restructuring the basic ways they deliver services to their patients, clients, audience, consumers. If you agree that we are in a time of change, then how can what volunteers do remain the same? Your crystal ball is just as valid as mine, but I predict that we will see totally new forms of volunteer support in the years to come. I emphasize this point in the introduction to this book because, more than anything, I hope the reader will come away with the conviction that it is right to be *proactive* in engaging the best, most qualified volunteers in service delivery. As with all other aspects of agency management, the time spent planning for volunteers is paid back richly by the results. Envision a place in which members of the community will gladly give their time to help meet a shared mission of service, and you will take all the right steps to make that the reality of your organization.

WHY VOLUNTEERS?

When Energize, Inc. conducts training seminars, we often include a session to examine and articulate the underlying assumptions of volunteer involvement. We present a list of key questions all leaders of volunteers should go home and ask—regardless of how old or new their volunteer program is. The first—and most critical—question is: "*Why* do we want volunteers?" This question is absolutely basic, yet it catches some people by surprise. Isn't the answer obvious? No. Aren't agencies "supposed" to have volunteers? Not necessarily. Hasn't our organization "always had" volunteers? So what?

As the executive, why *do* you want volunteers? Well, one answer always seems to be "because we do not have sufficient resources (money, staff, or whatever) to do our job without the help of volunteers." Unfortunately, while this response may be accurate, it also is a rather negative statement about volunteers. The implied corollary is that if there was sufficient money, or staff, or whatever, then volunteers would *not* be necessary. This makes volunteers a *second choice* resource.

I submit that this reasoning is at the root of a lot of the problems agencies have in activating volunteers and in working successfully with them. Recruitment based on "we don't have enough resources, so we are forced to turn to you" is not positive. Neither is supervision by salaried staff based on "I wish I had a paid helper, but I have to settle for you."

There are indeed some *first choice* reasons for wanting to attract volunteers—reasons that have nothing to do with the presence or absence of money. In our workshops, we ask trainees to imagine a "utopia" in which organizations such as theirs would have all the money in the world with which to do anything they please: offer one-to-one client service, pay for all types of consultation, take the staff on a retreat to Bermuda, etc. Here is the "exercise" question we pose: Given such a "utopia," would your agency still utilize volunteers in some way?

It generally takes several minutes for participants to be able to sort out their reactions to this question. And they find it hard to answer, at least at first. Some people honestly admit—with some relief—that they would not involve volunteers anymore. Others get sidetracked in observing that some people would still want to offer their services as volunteers—but we quickly point out that just because some people would always want to *be* volunteers does not mean that every agency would have to create an assignment for them. So the exercise has to take the *agency's* perspective only.

First Choice Reasons   After some lively discussion, the following are finally identified as being the unique things volunteers offer an organization—so special to volunteers that paying a salary negates or changes them completely:

- Volunteers have **credibility because they are unsalaried**. Paid staff are always perceived as "spokespeople" with a degree of *vested interest* in the outcome of a legislative hearing or funding proposal, since their livelihood depends upon the outcome. Volunteers, because their motivation is not profit-oriented, are seen by donors, clients, legislators, and the public as more objective and even as more sincere. This is what makes them such an asset in advocacy, public education, and fundraising.

  Note that this perception of volunteers as having no vested interest sometimes has nothing to do with the truth. For example, if a volunteer's grandmother founded the organization, then s/he has a different form of "vested interest"! Also, if a volunteer has been on the board for twenty years, objectivity may be questionable. But the fact remains that the *perception* and *assumption* of the listener or recipient are that the volunteer is more credible.

- Another version of credibility is that receiving assistance from a volunteer (rather than from an employee) **makes a difference to the recipient**. Many consumers are distrustful of paid service providers and are therefore more likely to believe and follow a volunteer's suggestions.

   In some circumstances, the important factor is the feeling that the volunteer is doing the task willingly—voluntarily—while the salaried staff are simply "doing a job." This is why prisoners, for example, are more willing to talk with volunteer visitors than with guards or state social workers. It is why patients in hospitals are more cheered by the visit of a volunteer than a nurse: volunteers demonstrate that neighbors have not forgotten them nor are "turned off" by their illness. Nurses, on the other hand, must provide service, regardless of their personal feelings about the patient.

   Finally, some programs such as one-to-one home visitation or Big Brothers/Big Sisters would change radically in their purpose without volunteers. If we salary a Big Brother, we give the child another babysitter. The very word "brother" in the volunteer's title indicates that the service is not based on its being a "job." The same idea is at work with the title of "friendly visitor." You don't pay a friend to visit.

   For your agency, the service recipient's comfort level with a volunteer may elicit feedback or other information not as easily obtained by an employee.

- Volunteers are **insider/outsiders.** While your paid staff may well live nearby, volunteers are usually considered "community representatives" even if they are neighbors of your employees. This is because most employees approach their jobs from a specific professional perspective and may be too close to the work to "see the forest for the trees." Volunteers, on the other hand, bring a wide range of professional and other backgrounds. Because they give a few hours at time, volunteers have a broader point of view. They still think like a member of the public but have also made a commitment to your agency, so you can count on their distinct input.

- Volunteers extend your **sphere of influence** and access to additional people, businesses and organizations in the community. Even the volunteer who helps you once a year becomes another person with knowledge about your work. This ripple effect can spread increased good will, in that happy volunteers will speak well of the organization to others. (This is a two-edged sword, of course, because unhappy volunteers can create bad will for you, too.)

- Volunteers are valuable as **objective policy makers** and (even in the wealthy utopia scenario) are therefore necessary as members of nonprofit boards of directors. Boards are—by law—an intermediary between donors/funders and program participants, acting as "trustees" of funds from which they themselves derive no profit. Since the ultimate power of a board is the decision to close an agency, it is clear that such decision-making should be done by people who are not personally affected by such an action nor by less drastic measures such as cutting some programs. Also, the objectivity of volunteers is aided by not being on-site full time. Distance provides perspective.

- Volunteers bring the **luxury of focus**. Paid staff must equitably share their time among all service recipients or a full caseload. Not so volunteers. They have the option to focus intensively on a particular issue or client, even to the exclusion of extraneous tasks. Volunteers can specialize. This is a luxury of concentration and time not normally justifiable for employees, while volunteers can actually be recruited to provide such individualized attention to one task. (You can even recruit three volunteers to work with one client, if necessary.)

- Volunteers are more **free to criticize** than are salaried staff. Again, this is a function of being outside the career-ladder, promotion-seeking concerns that are often legitimate for employees.

- Because volunteers are not dependent upon the organization for their livelihood, they can approach assignments with **less pressure and stress**, often an asset in accomplishing the tasks to be done.

- Because volunteers are always **"private citizens,"** they are free to contact legislators or the media in a way employees may not be permitted to do (because of possible limitations on legislative activity by such regulations as the Hatch Act). Though this is yet another two-edged sword (i.e., the volunteer may use this access to speak against you), it means that volunteers can be powerful advocates.

  Similarly, though volunteers act as "agents" of your organization, they have more flexibility in cutting through some of the red tape of bureaucratic systems, political boundaries, and other artificial barriers. This is increasingly critical in work with an international component. Volunteers—as private citizens with a mission—can make contacts, travel across borders, and promote cooperation in ways that governments find almost impossible.

- Volunteers can **experiment** with new ideas and service approaches that are not yet ready to be funded—or that no one wants to fund for a wide variety of reasons. Historically, in fact, volunteers have always been the pioneers in creating new services (and ultimately new paid jobs), often against the tide of opposition from more traditional institutions.

There is one additional "first choice" reason for involving volunteers that does, in fact, involve money. But it must be worded correctly. Too often, in an effort to praise the contributions of volunteers, executives (and legislators) say: "Volunteers save us money!" They may even calculate a total dollar value for these supposed "savings." In Chapter 11, we will discuss the dollar value of volunteers at length. For now, however, understand that volunteers never "save" money. Do you have money available that you did not have to spend because you utilized volunteers? Hardly. Much more accurate is the recognition that volunteers *allow you to spend every dollar you have—and then do more.* Volunteers **extend the budget**.

Implications   What does all this imply? Well, first
it shows that there are definitely
areas in which volunteers—
because they are volunteers—can
be even more effective than salaried staff. Second it raises the
question of whether your agency is maximizing these "first
choice" areas. Specifically, in your organization:

> —Are volunteers being used as legislative advocates? as
> fundraisers? as public educators? in any role that makes
> use of their credibility?

> —Are volunteers providing direct service to consumers,
> especially in tasks that may benefit from a higher degree
> of comfort level or personalization?

> —Do you have a system for getting feedback from volun-
> teers? Are there channels for making suggestions or stat-
> ing criticisms?

> —Do you utilize volunteers to establish collaborative
> arrangements or to cut red tape in some way?

Examine the job descriptions volunteers are presently fulfilling in your setting and determine whether you are benefitting
as much as possible from the unique aspects of volunteer service.

So Why Pay a   Perhaps you have been thinking
Salary?   about the reverse of the question
of why you involve volunteers,
namely: "Why should we salary
anyone?" It is important (especially for this book) to recognize
that the answer is *not* that offering a salary gets you people with
better *qualifications*. A volunteer can be just as highly trained
and experienced as can any employee. Instead, offering a salary
gives the agency a **pre-determined number of work hours**
per week, the right to **dictate the employee's work schedule**,
a certain amount of **control** over the nature and priorities **of the
work to be done**, and **continuity**.

When you pay a salary, you can require that the person give your organization forty hours a week or whatever number is necessary. Because most people need to earn a living, people can rarely give one agency that much volunteer time per week.

In addition, volunteers are always free to select their individual work schedule. Though you can require volunteers to commit to a schedule and be dependable, a person does not usually jeopardize his/her volunteer position by telling you up front that s/he goes to Florida in February or that his/her schedule will change every semester to match a course roster. On the other hand, an employee can indeed be told exactly when the agency expects him or her to be present and can be made to submit vacation schedules, for example, for prior approval.

The area of "control" has many levels and will be discussed in more detail in Chapter 9. Some of what you may feel you have in the way of control over employees may be more mythical than real. For example, you really have no way of stopping an employee from going to the press with a story—though you can threaten termination of employment and hope the fear of being fired is a deterrent. The more realistic aspect of control is that you can dictate job assignments and expect the employee to fulfill these, even if s/he dislikes the task or even disagrees with it. Further, you can set the priorities within which the employee must emphasize certain tasks over others. A volunteer always retains *freedom of choice* and can refuse to work on a project for various reasons, without losing the opportunity to volunteer in another assignment.

Finally, a salaried position provides continuity for the organization. Even if the person filling the position changes over time, the function itself remains relatively stable. The public and the rest of staff can expect a certain standard in the way the service is provided by that position.

Recognize that your organization has made choices throughout its development about whether to accomplish work with volunteers or to hire paid staff, or to mesh the two. There are, after all, examples of all-volunteer groups providing a multitude of community services. It was probably your volunteer founders who raised the first funds to pay salaries. And when you are faced with a budget crisis, the question of who should do what surfaces again. This whole subject of the reasons for one set of workers versus another, and the need for mutual understanding of abilities and limitations, is so critical to the success of a volunteer program that we will return to it in several chapters.

Other Benefits of Volunteers

As we have seen, there are some clear "first choice" reasons for utilizing volunteers, even in an all-the-money-in-the-world utopia. And there are good reasons for salarying some workers, too. Since we live in the real, limited-resources world, what are the other benefits to an organization for involving volunteers? Volunteers offer:

- Extra hands and the potential to do more than could be done simply with limited salaried staff; this "more" might mean an increased amount of service, expanded hours of operation, or different/new types of services.

- Diversity; volunteers may be different from the salaried staff in terms of age, race, social background, income, educational level, etc. This translates into many more points of view and perhaps even a sort of checks and balances to the danger of the staff becoming myopic or inbred.

- Skills that augment the ones employees already possess. Ideally volunteers are recruited exactly because the salaried staff cannot have every skill or talent necessary to do all aspects of the job. These skills can be very concrete such as being bilingual, knowing how to dry herbs, or being able to produce a newsletter. Or, they can be less tangible such as being able to relate to teenagers or the homeless.

- Community ownership of solutions to mutual problems. Especially if your organization addresses issues affecting the quality of life, when people participate as volunteers they empower themselves to improve their own neighborhood (which is your mission, after all). In government agencies, citizen participation enacts the principle of government "by the people."

- Advocacy for adequate funding. Volunteers know the value of full-time, paid staff and are often in the best position to understand why your organization needs more money in addition to volunteers.

In addition to all of the above, studies have shown that satisfied volunteers frequently are so supportive of the organizations with which they serve that they become donors of money and goods as well. They also support special events and fundraisers by attending themselves and bringing along family and friends. In the case of cultural arts organizations, volunteers thereby help to expand the audience or public for performances and exhibitions.

Putting These Benefits to Work

As you begin or expand your organization's volunteer component you (or your director of volunteers) will be assessing the needs that volunteers might fill. Being clear on why you want volunteer involvement (the benefits we have just listed) will help to identify specific volunteer job descriptions.

The wrong question to ask when trying to define volunteer assignments is: "What could a volunteer do to help us?" The answer is generally tainted by the staff's (and your) stereotypes about who might be recruited. If you envision a little old lady in a flowered hat and tennis shoes, then you will give a very limited response to the question of what such a volunteer could do for you!

The more meaningful question is: "What needs to be done?" This has some sub-categories, such as:

—What are we doing now that we would like to do more of?

—What unmet needs do our clients have that we presently can do nothing about?

—What unmet needs does the staff have (to support them in their work)?

—What might we do differently if we had more skills or time available to us?

The answers to these questions will provide a wide range of possible assignments. Not every idea will be appropriate to implement with a volunteer, but the door will be open to creative and challenging assignments.

It is fundamental that the kinds of volunteers you will attract are directly connected to what you want them to do. If every volunteer position is an "aide," don't be surprised if less-skilled people offer their help. Conversely, if the assignments require special talents and leadership abilities, prospective volunteers who have that skill level will gravitate towards working with you.

Don't Miss Opportunities

Sometimes the challenge will be to make the most of unexpected opportunities. Imagine your delighted and positive reaction if a businessman would contact your office and, completely unsolicited, offer you a donation of $10,000. Now picture a slightly different scenario: the same businessman contacts your office, unsolicited, and explains that he has taken early retirement and hopes to become a volunteer with a worthwhile organization. He has a lifetime of proven business success and wants to contribute a minimum of two days a week of his time. What's your reaction now?

In the past year two retired friends have coincidentally asked for my help in finding meaningful volunteer work to do. Neither of them (they don't know each other) have yet found a volunteer placement that suits them. The problem is that they can't seem to find an agency willing to create a position to tap their skills. Even worse, they have yet to feel welcomed or appreciated for their offer of contributed time.

These men are 55 to 65 years old, college educated, with a wealth of management experience. They also have been financial donors to a range of community organizations over the years. To be truthful, neither is particularly well-informed about the realities of nonprofit life nor about the issues and problems of the clientele of most human service agencies. They undoubtedly feel that nonprofits are generally poorly managed by well-meaning novices. In other words, to put these men to work effectively as volunteers will require the right balance of respect and training. But it would seem that the rewards would be worth the effort because these men intend to stick with any commitment made.

Independently, my two friends have experienced frustration, dismissal, and rejection from a combined total of ten organizations so far. Their first challenge is getting in the door. When they call an agency and explain what they want to do, they are often referred to the executive director's office—even when there is a director of volunteers. This is because receptionists sense that the contact is at a higher level than "ordinary" volunteer candidates (an indicator of the impression the staff has formed of the present volunteer program). So the executive takes the call, but is at a loss as to how to respond. Does the gentleman mean that he wants to be considered for the board? No? Well, now, we'll have to think about what we might be able to do with you. Can we call you back? (Several have not.)

Most organizations are unprepared for the unexpected offer of help, particularly if the prospective volunteer is highly skilled. The technical assistance, consultation, or project management that volunteers such as my friends can provide would truly be unaffordable to most nonprofits, yet the effort required to make such a placement work seems insurmountable to many. It may even seem a bit threatening. But you can learn to think of unexpected volunteer expertise like a "designated gift" that gives you the opportunity to move forward on plans that no one else has the time or perhaps the talent to do right now.

How clear are you on your organization's capability to respond to unusually-qualified volunteer applicants? It does take planning and some staff training to be open to a more challenging type of volunteer. But consider another potential consequence of turning such people away: how likely will they be to give money to an agency that is disinterested in anything but their checkbooks? So here's an even more interesting question: when was the last time you actively sought people to contribute sophisticated expertise? If you only look for cash, you may well be missing the boat.

As CEO, you have a role to play in making sure that employees brainstorm creatively in finding ways for talented volunteers to become involved. Help employees avoid "dumping" on volunteers all the tasks they find distasteful or low level. While it is wonderful if a volunteer can be recruited who enjoys the things the employee dislikes, thereby pleasing them both, this approach backfires if the employee never intends to share any of the tasks that are more challenging or rewarding.

Once you have a sense of the kinds of needs you want volunteers to meet, you are ready to consider the practical aspects of implementing a volunteer program.

CONSIDERATIONS
IN PLANNING

From the perspective of human resource management, it is clear that the volunteer program is the nonsalaried personnel department of the agency. What does this mean in practice?

If you were given a donation today for $100,000, with the stipulation that it be spent on salaries for new employees, you would know exactly how to proceed effectively. You would probably follow a sequence of tasks very much like this:

—assess the agency's needs and pinpoint where new employees would be most useful;

—develop job descriptions, including the qualifications you'd look for in applicants;

—publicize the openings;

—interview and screen applicants, with the expectation that you will have to turn away some candidates in your search for the best people;

—select the people you will hire and match them to the available openings;

—orient these new employees to the policies and practices of the agency;

—train these new employees in the specifics of the job to which each has been assigned;

—find a place for them to work.

Once the new employees were on board, you would then be concerned about their supervision, in-service training, and periodic performance evaluation. As top administrator, you'd recognize that if any one of these personnel management steps is omitted or done without high standards, effective, quality delivery of service is jeopardized.

The premise of this book is that every one of these tasks is equally pertinent to the effective utilization of *volunteers*. If you accept this premise, the following are ways to plan for the integration of volunteers into your organization.

Statement of Philosophy

We have already considered the question of "why do we want volunteers?" Once you have identified exactly why *your* organization wishes to involve volunteers, it is very helpful to develop a written "Statement of Philosophy" expressing your point of view. This statement can be useful in a number of ways, especially for establishing clear relationships between volunteers and salaried staff, for recruiting new volunteers, and for demonstrating appreciation of citizen involvement. The Statement of Philosophy then becomes the basis or framework upon which you and the board of directors can develop goals, policies and other decisions affecting volunteers in the organization.

When drafting a Statement of Philosophy, it is important to be specific about why you are involving volunteers. For example, a statement that says only, "volunteers will assist in the achievement of agency goals," is insufficient. Similarly, a statement that limits roles, such as "volunteers will supplement, not supplant, paid staff" also does not do the trick. Though this latter sentiment has been gospel in some quarters, it is too limiting. For example, why must volunteers only "supplement"? Why can't they "innovate," or "experiment," or "work parallel to"? None of these roles diminish the importance of the function of the paid staff.

A better approach to the Statement of Philosophy would be something like this:

Our agency encourages the teamwork of employees and volunteers so that we can offer our consumers the best services possible. Volunteers contribute their unique talents, skills, and knowledge of our community to provide personalized attention to consumers, enable the salaried staff to concentrate on the work for which they were trained, and educate the public about our organization and its cause.

In a government agency (whether national, state or local), the role of "citizen participation" deserves clarification in such a Statement of Philosophy. Here is one way to express political commitment to teamwork between civil servants and citizen volunteers.

In a residential facility such as a nursing home, the Statement of Philosophy could include something about the interrelationship of the volunteers, paid staff, and the residents themselves. For example, you might state the desire of the agency to encourage residents to participate fully in the activities that create a home environment for all residents.

If you are recruiting volunteers for a profit-making enterprise, it is vital to specify that volunteers will be assigned mainly to the personalized, direct client services for which volunteers are uniquely suited.

It should come as no surprise that good volunteer management requires the setting of goals and objectives for the achievements of **Goals and Objectives**
the volunteer program. There is no reason to let abounding gratitude for donated volunteer time restrain an organization from setting standards of achievement. In fact, volunteers usually prefer to have some way to assess their service contribution.

In developing initial and then ongoing goals and objectives, bigger is not always better. There are other ways to measure the successful impact of volunteers than to point to having "more" volunteers this year than last year. The simple addition of more people into the volunteer program does not self-evidently mean better service delivery. Numerical goals of "how many" volunteers to bring on board are meaningless unless serious expectations of productivity are also articulated. In fact, the number of volunteers needed is a *strategy* for attaining what you want volunteers to produce. (Some organizations would be more effective if they cut their present volunteer force in half and concentrated instead on recruiting fewer people with higher qualifications.)

Just as with employees, it is possible to monitor and measure the accomplishments of volunteers by stating goals and objectives at the beginning of a period—and then assessing whether these were achieved. In formulating goals and objectives for the volunteer program, you might consider such questions as:

—What do we expect individual volunteers to accomplish in each job category?

—What ethnic and cultural diversity do we want represented in our volunteer program?

—What kinds of skills would we like volunteers to bring to our services?

—What reaction do we want our consumers to have to the service they receive from volunteers?

—What effect do we want volunteers to have in special assignments, such as public education, public relations, etc.?

—What outreach efforts do we expect our director of volunteers to make this year?

Goals and objectives set for the volunteer component should correlate with the overall goals and objectives of the agency. Recently I conducted a management retreat with the department heads of a large hospital system. In preparation, the CEO sent me an impressive 80-page "Five-Year Strategic Plan" for the institution. I dutifully read the entire document and when I arrived at the retreat asked why—despite the current participation of almost 600 volunteers—there was not one word about volunteers in the strategic plan! After much consternation, it became clear that neither the administrators nor their outside consultant had considered it possible to "plan" for volunteers!

As with absolutely every other aspect of organizational life, the amount of time you spend determining what you want volunteer involvement to be will directly affect the quality and creativity of what you get. Ignore this aspect of your organization and maybe you'll get lucky. But if you incorporate planning for volunteers into overall agency planning, you will naturally take the steps necessary to assure that you reach those goals.

Remember also to include volunteers in your plans for future agency projects. If, for example, you are proposing a new community outreach effort that will be under the auspices of the public relations department, and you expect to train volunteers as speakers in that effort, develop a written objective for this. After all, if you wanted the community outreach project to develop a film, you would certainly include an objective relating to the work of the audiovisual department. As CEO, you have the responsibility for inserting an objective relating to volunteer utilization into the plans for any appropriate project and, as we will discuss later, for involving the person in charge of the volunteer program in such overall agency planning.

Policy Setting

Throughout this book you will recognize issues that can be solved or avoided by setting policy in advance that everyone understands. Since you and the board of directors (volunteers themselves, of course) are responsible for developing and implementing policy, you have the authority to set the rules for volunteer involvement. When people understand the rules, they can either follow them or work to change them. But without rules in place, everyone operates independently—and you have no way of enforcing standards.

Each of the chapters in this book suggests an area requiring policy decisions. It is a policy decision to recruit volunteers in the first place, and to allocate resources to their support. Make the effort to identify existing policy gaps, especially in terms of the interaction between volunteers and salaried staff. Be sure all new (and veteran) employees know the standards you have set and be alert to new situations which require revision of policies about volunteers.

The setting—and then the enforcing—of policies involving volunteers are two of the most visible ways you can demonstrate commitment to the integration of volunteers into your organization.

The Role of the Board The subject of volunteers belongs in the board room, but it is too rarely raised there.[1] Boards of directors should exercise the same legal and fiduciary stewardship with volunteers as with any other organization resource. Apart from the things we have already been discussing, volunteers are a legitimate subject of concern to a board of directors because volunteers are the result of "people raising" just as cash is the result of "fund raising." Both are valuable resources to the organization and both are "development" issues.

Basic data about volunteers should be reported to the board along with other organizational information. The point is not to manage daily activities, but to observe patterns over time. Volunteers are part of the full picture, to be integrated into other organization decision-making. Here are some board-level questions:

—Is it desirable for the volunteer corps to reflect or represent the community and/or consumers we serve? Do we need an affirmative action statement for volunteer recruitment?

—What are the pros and cons of adapting our volunteer involvement to the emerging new trends and issues in volunteerism? What criteria should we employ to determine which trends to pursue?

—Have we taken all the risk management steps necessary to protect the client, the volunteer, and the paid staff? (See Chapter 9.)

—Do we want to develop collaborative arrangements with existing community groups and is volunteer action one way to accomplish this?

—What are the ways we might try to support new service initiatives, in addition to cash? As we attempt to raise the needed money, are we making the attempt to raise the needed volunteers?

Schedule time on the board agenda to discuss volunteers. Even if this only happens once a year, the status of volunteers increases when they become a formal part of the board's agenda.

Where You Are Now

As already indicated, you may be the executive of an organization at any stage of its volunteer program development. However, you may find yourself wanting to fill in the planning gaps overlooked in the past. If you already have volunteers on site, be sure to involve them as much as possible in helping to define their situation. Forming an ad hoc planning team of current volunteers may be one way to do some of the work necessary to define the program structure. Such a team also allows volunteers genuine participation in the program. After all, you are formulating policies and procedures that will affect them (and may change some of the ways they operate now). What better way to show that you, as CEO, value volunteer input than to ask them for advice?

If you have decided to involve volunteers for the first time, analyze your organization to see if "bootlegged" volunteers are already active. For example, have you been asking neighboring church groups to help you once a year with a special event? Are friends and relatives of service recipients (or the board, or the staff) allowed to "help out" if they are interested? Are students given the chance to do internships? You may discover that you already have quite a list of "volunteers," though you may not have identified them as such in the past. You need to know if you are starting from scratch or indeed have a base of community supporters upon which to build. This identification process can be pleasantly revealing.

Starting Small

No matter what your ultimate goals for volunteer involvement are, it is good management practice to start small. Pilot test new volunteer assignment categories, allowing time to work out the procedural details that will only surface once a volunteer is on the job. Give salaried staff the chance to learn how to work successfully with volunteers and add more people only as the support structure develops.

Perhaps you can select one or two units of the agency in which to begin placing volunteers, expanding to the other units over time.

Management Options   Each reader will come to this book under different circumstances. You may be operating in an agency in which there is already a highly-structured and well-managed volunteer component, or you may be considering starting a volunteer program for the first time. You may be the head of a large institution or the only salaried staff member among a multitude of volunteers. Whatever your situation, you will have to make some choices as to how you wish to begin or continue involving volunteers. Some management options are:

> *Model I:* You, as head of the organization, lead the volunteer program and personally supervise volunteers just as you do paid staff.

> *Model II:* You designate a leader for the volunteer "program" and all volunteers are recruited and supervised by this "Director of Volunteers."

> *Model III:* The volunteer program is "decentralized," in that all staff recruit and supervise volunteers active in their particular units.

> *Model IV:* A mixture of models II and III, in which you designate a Director of Volunteers who recruits and administers volunteers, but deploys them to whichever units need assistance; day-to-day supervision is given by the line staff.

> *Model V:* Volunteers are self-led, generally organized with elected officers, etc.

Model IV is the most common management option, but there are still more choices to make in determining the leadership of volunteers. An entire chapter will be devoted to staffing the volunteer program, but your first major decision is whether to designate an existing member of the salaried staff to head the volunteer program in addition to his or her other responsibilities (possibly yourself), or whether to create a new part-time or full-time employee position of director of volunteers.

Organizational Placement

Whatever management option you choose, to whom will you have the person in charge of volunteers report? This decision impacts on your entire chain of command and sends a message to all employees and volunteers. In a later chapter, we will consider the question of supervision of the leader of volunteers more fully but, for now, recognize that where you place the head of the program implies where—even whether—volunteers themselves are integrated into the organization.

There is no "correct" place for the director of volunteers on the organizational chart. Each setting is different and parameters such as agency size, job descriptions of other staff members, etc. will affect your decision. However, be aware that whoever supervises the director of volunteers must truly understand the things that make that position unique (see Chapter 4). For example, if you place the volunteer program under the public relations department, will the director of public relations be able to assist the director of volunteers in her/his responsibilities related to the daily operations of the agency? Generally, a PR department has no role in in-house service delivery or activities. Conversely, if the director of volunteers is placed under, say, the casework supervisor, will that person be supportive of the volunteer program's public outreach efforts? Again, the casework supervisor would normally have no reason to do public speaking, etc.

It is useful to consider the connection between the director of volunteers and the agency's director of human resources or personnel. There are both similarities and differences between these two positions. Structurally, as already noted, they both recruit and place workers into your organization. Both require policies and guidelines to clarify expectations of paid and volunteer personnel. But the director of volunteers generally is much more involved in day-to-day agency activities and has many more community responsibilities as well.

In reality, the director of volunteers is a *separate, independent department head,* in that s/he has responsibilities substantially different from, though linked to, all other departments, and in that s/he supervises a large cadre of workers, albeit volunteers. Ideally, the director of volunteers should answer directly to you. This also sends a message to the *volunteers.* It says that they have a direct line to the top decision maker. It conveys a similar message to all employees: volunteers are a subject of daily interest to the top executive. When you consider that the volunteer program is the agency's nonsalaried personnel department and that you, as CEO, are responsible for the deployment of all human resources, the decision to place the director of volunteers directly under you is more than justifiable.

If you are the executive of a very large organization, the director of volunteers may have to report to you through a vice-president or some other key administrator. Again, recognize the messages you send to everyone through your choice of where to place the volunteer program. Consider the other organizational units answering to the same administrator and assess whether there is an evident rationale for placing the volunteer program alongside these other units—or whether the placement implies that volunteers are a "miscellaneous" agency function.

Organizational Chart

Does your present organizational chart include volunteers? Take out the chart you show to funding sources or to new employees. Are volunteers mentioned on it at all? To begin with, if you are with a voluntary agency, are the members of your board of directors noted? They should be at the top of your hierarchy, shouldn't they? Do you have an advisory council or a fundraising body such as an auxiliary? Are these volunteers visible on the chart? Now what about frontline volunteers?

The main, and therefore priority, work of each employee is generally reflected on an organizational chart. So if you have a "director of volunteers," that position is probably shown. But if the person responsible for volunteers holds a different title because volunteer management is only a small part of his/her job, is the function of volunteer management shown on the chart at all? If not, where does this leave volunteers? Are they out of sight/out of mind?

Whether an organization has a designated director of volunteers or someone doing the work part-time, it is probable that that individual will appear on the chart as an employee. But too often volunteers themselves are not indicated at all. If they are shown, they frequently are placed under the head of the volunteer program in this misleading way:

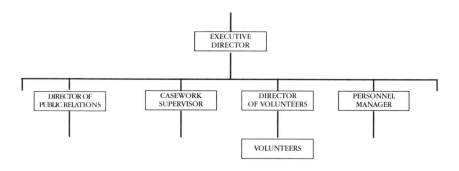

Why does such a chart send a misleading message? It implies that volunteers "belong" to the director of volunteers and effectively lets all other salaried staff off the hook in caring about volunteers. Yet if you have a personnel department, do you place one box saying "all employees" under it? Of course not. Only payroll clerks and others who are directly supervised by the personnel manager are shown "under" him or her, while all other employees are shown under the departments in which they are placed. The volunteer department works in exactly the same way—channeling volunteers to the appropriate units where daily supervision is provided. So a more accurate organizational chart might look like the illustration on the next page.

Sometimes CEOs are reluctant to create such an organizational chart in the fear that funding sources will incorrectly conclude that the agency has sufficient resources. It seems somehow dishonest to show so many "staff." One way to handle this is to make sure the chart is labeled as a *functional* organizational chart, not as simply a list of employed staff. Then you can indicate employees by circles or squares, and volunteers by a differently shaped "box." Or use solid and dotted lines.

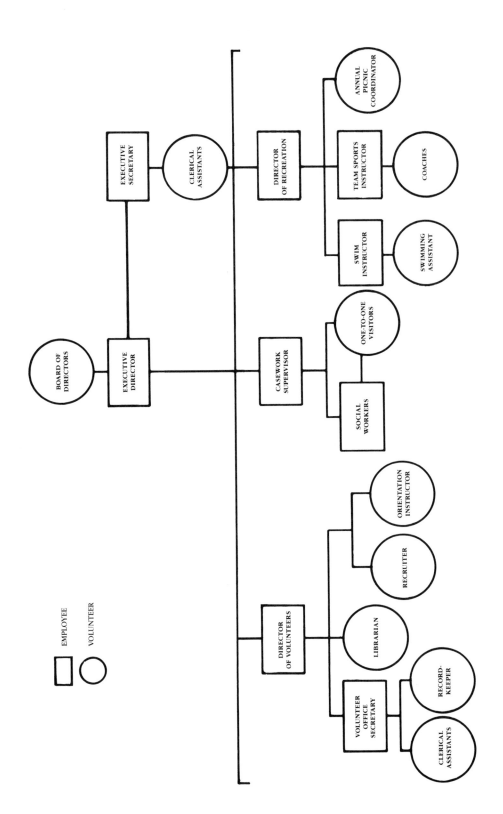

EMPLOYEE

VOLUNTEER

BOARD OF DIRECTORS

EXECUTIVE DIRECTOR

EXECUTIVE SECRETARY

CLERICAL ASSISTANTS

DIRECTOR OF RECREATION

TEAM SPORTS INSTRUCTOR

ANNUAL PICNIC COORDINATOR

COACHES

SWIM INSTRUCTOR

SWIMMING ASSISTANT

CASEWORK SUPERVISOR

ONE-TO-ONE VISITORS

SOCIAL WORKERS

DIRECTOR OF VOLUNTEERS

ORIENTATION INSTRUCTOR

RECRUITER

LIBRARIAN

VOLUNTEER OFFICE SECRETARY

RECORD-KEEPER

CLERICAL ASSISTANTS

One more point: always use *titles* when referring to volunteers—and don't feel that you have to keep the adjective "volunteer" in the title. If a volunteer is coordinating your alumni drive, then s/he is the Alumni Drive Coordinator—does it matter what the salary is or isn't?

Agency Image

One more consideration in planning for volunteers is to be sure your "house is in order" before opening the doors to recruit help from members of the public. While no one expects an organization to function perfectly or to have superhuman staff members, volunteers are affected by internal agency problems. If the staff squabbles or is disorganized, volunteers will be caught in the middle.

The ability to recruit volunteers is strongly and directly connected to your organization's image in the community. If your services are viewed negatively for any reason, it will be hard to attract good volunteers (though people will respond positively to a request to help make things better). On the other hand, if the public sees your agency effectively filling a need, it will be easier to encourage volunteers to join you.

Having no image or visibility in the community poses similar recruitment problems. If people are unclear about what it is you do (which might be furthered by a confusing agency name), then you or your leader of volunteers will first have to conduct a generalized public relations effort before you can concentrate on the specifics of volunteer recruitment. After all, how can someone be expected to offer you service if s/he doesn't know what you do?

Mergers

Whether out of concern for more stable funding or to respond to evolving community needs, we are seeing an increase in mergers between similar or compatible organizations. Mergers always mean turmoil in the short run, even if ultimately successful. And the more agencies or sites involved, the greater the numbers of people caught in uncertainty, resistance and fear—even if coupled with hope and gratification.

Volunteers are frequently among the people coping with the effects of a merger, yet are rarely part of the plan. In many cases, volunteers committed themselves to the particular agency now perhaps losing its identity under the merger. Where do their loyalties belong? The reorganization sure to come may include the elimination of staff jobs seen as duplicative. Will this happen to volunteer assignments too? Is anyone in a decision-making position thinking about this?

Some mergers have resulted in the attempted consolidation of several pre-existing volunteer programs, often with the creation of one central office at one site only. In some situations this may be quite workable. But in others it signals the beginning of the end of a thriving volunteer force at the other sites. Unlike employees who want to save their jobs and will hang on during the changes of a transition period, volunteers need to feel that their services are wanted and useful each time they come in. When everything is in flux and then the familiar director of volunteers is laid off, it is understandable that some volunteers will leave in frustration.

The key point is that, if you are anticipating or undergoing a merger, put the subject of volunteers on the agenda. Talk with volunteers themselves and learn their hopes and fears. Ask their advice for how to restructure the volunteer program, assuring them continuity within change. If you must consolidate the volunteer office at one site, designate someone at the other sites to be at least the official staff liaison for volunteers, even if this is an interim plan. Demonstrate that you are taking the needs of volunteers into consideration.

If there are two or more independently-run associations such as auxiliaries or friends groups, it may be unrealistic to expect them to merge as well, at least not immediately. There may even be advantages to retaining a circle of support for each site. Again, the worst strategy is to ignore the issue or to expect the groups to "work it out" by themselves. You want to send the message that they matter to your organization and that you will work with them to find the best solution for everyone.

Backing Up the Plan   In this chapter we have examined areas requiring thoughtful planning and preparation. In the next chapter we'll talk about money. Successful volunteer involvement necessitates not only the allocating of funds, but also providing access to other organizational resources.

[1]Summarized from a fuller discussion in *The Board's Role in Effective Volunteer Involvement* by Susan J. Ellis, The National Center for Nonprofit Boards, 1995.

BUDGETING AND ALLOCATING RESOURCES

Volunteers are not "free" labor. They are a human resource that costs substantially less in hard cash than any other resource, but funds, space, supplies and other materials must be allocated to support the work of volunteers. The "cost effectiveness" of such allocations is easy to prove: the expenses incurred by a volunteer component are "leverage" money that translates into contribution of services valued at many multiples of the original expenditure. Later, we'll look at what that value of volunteer service really is—and how to compute it.

Avoid the mistake of seeing the volunteer program as "small" simply because there are few salaried staff assigned to it. Though personnel costs may be low, the volunteer program's budget needs in other categories can be substantial because of the additional people being put to work.

Let's examine each possible line item in a volunteer program budget and discuss the considerations in arriving at a reasonable dollar figure. Special needs in the start-up phase of a program will be indicated in each category. At the end of this chapter is a worksheet that provides space for you to calculate anticipated expenses in each line item described here.

PERSONNEL

As you review the expenditures necessary in the personnel category, consider both direct and indirect costs. As we will be discussing in the chapter on staffing, the number of full or part-time staff you designate or hire will depend upon many factors, including the number and types of volunteers in the program, hours of operation, etc.

Energize is often asked about the appropriate "salary range" for a director of volunteers. This is an unproductive question because of the vast variety of settings in which volunteer programs operate. It is nearly impossible to compare the operating budgets of an institution such as a museum with a grass-roots agency such as a literacy program. Clearly the "salary range" for any position, including the top executive, will differ wildly between such extremely diverse situations.

Determining the salary of your director of volunteers should be based on one criterion only:

> *What are you presently paying other department heads or key administrative employees?*

The director of volunteers is a management position and the only valid measure of appropriate salary is in comparison with other positions at the same level in your agency. In fact, this is one indicator of how much value you place on the position and, ultimately, on the importance of the contribution of volunteers. This job requires decision-making, leadership, and a great deal of public contact on behalf of the agency. If you place the salary on a level with line or clerical staff, you cannot demand management-level credentials or performance. You should therefore budget for the position on the basis of its professionalism—and hire accordingly!

The personnel budget category will, of course, include the program's secretary and any additional assistants necessary because of the size or schedule of the program. Employee benefits are the next line item.

You might want to estimate the cost of the time devoted by other agency staff to the training and supervision of volunteers. While this will not be a direct budget line item, it may help you in identifying the true value of the resources you are allocating to support volunteers.

OPERATIONAL COSTS AND
OTHER NEEDED RESOURCES

Several of the following items will not be new expenses but will require a re-allocation of present organizational resources.

Space and Other Facilities

The volunteer program needs office space that affords the following:

—Easy access from the entrance of the building, since prospective volunteers (members of the public) will be coming in for interviews. Also, proximity to the entrance will allow the director of volunteers to maintain contact with volunteers arriving and departing on their scheduled work days (e.g., permitting control of the sign in/out system).

—Privacy for interviewing prospective volunteers.

—Secure storage space for volunteers' coats and other personal belongings (and uniforms, if applicable).

—Group work space for meetings or collating of materials.

It is not always stating the obvious to note that each volunteer also needs adequate space in which to work. Staff may indeed want assistance with a variety of projects, but has anyone thought through *where* the volunteer will sit, have a clear surface, have access to office equipment? Also, is there anywhere that the volunteer can *store* his or her work materials in-between visits? Is there any provision for a mail bin or file folder so that messages may be left for the volunteer? These kinds of details make work go smoothly and indicate that volunteers are indeed integrated into the organizational environment.

In addition to the space needed on a daily basis, the volunteer office also needs access to:

—Space for orientation sessions and in-service training meetings (varying group sizes).

—Adequate rest room facilities. (Remember, the numbers of volunteers entering the building daily may be high enough to put a strain on your existing facilities. The school system in Anchorage, Alaska faced this exact problem when teachers in hurriedly-erected "Quonset hut" elementary school buildings refused to allow volunteers to utilize the toilets in the "faculty lounges." It turned out that these lounges only contained "one-seaters" and that an extra twenty or so adults per day genuinely caused a rest room line for the teachers. This is a great example of lack of *planning!*)

—Space in various locations for sign-in books or other volunteer communication mechanisms, such as bulletin boards.

—Possibly, lounge areas for volunteer rest periods.

Furniture and Equipment

Assess available work space and furniture in terms of the impact of more people (volunteers) coming into the facility at various hours. Too many organizations have discovered too late that they did not have enough chairs for volunteers who dutifully arrived for work at their scheduled time.

Other needs (most of which are clearly one-time costs rather than annual expenses) are:

—coat racks

—computers or typewriters designated for volunteer use (especially if a number of volunteers have been recruited to do clerical work—it is usually not feasible to expect salaried secretaries to share their keyboards all the time)

—computer software designed for handling volunteer program data needs

—slide projector and screen, or VCR (for recruitment or volunteer orientation slide shows and videos)

—bulletin boards

—file cabinets (keep in mind that the volunteer office is the nonsalaried personnel office and will generate files in much the same way as the employee *personnel* office does)

—possibly some comfortable furniture for a conversation/interview or lounge area

Telephones

Again, the number of telephone instruments and lines will depend upon the size and nature of volunteer activities. But keep in mind that the volunteer office depends heavily on telephone contacts, both in recruitment/public relations and in ongoing communication with volunteers.

If you are creating any project that involves telephoning *by volunteers*—telephone reassurance programs, market surveying, political canvassing, client follow-up—the possible rise in cost of telephone calls may be a major consideration for you. With the changes in telephone company service still evolving, the budget line for telephone calls may increase in the future, even if local calls form the bulk of the contacts.

Supplies

This is a budget category that is too often treated as minor, while it is really the tip of an iceberg. Budgeting for supplies should be done on the basis of the needs of both the volunteer "office" and the volunteers themselves. Consumption of supplies will rise as the number of active volunteers increases: productivity comes at the cost of support materials. A possible list of supplies would include:

—paper and stationery
—pencils and pens
—typewriter and printer ribbons and similar supplies
—paper clips, erasers, etc.
—paper towels and other maintenance materials
—coffee, tea, and paper cups

In a workshop I ran for school principals, a participant asked to address his colleagues. He proceeded to tell the true story of his experience in the first year of inviting volunteers into his school. At the March faculty meeting, he admonished his teachers for having wastefully depleted the school's supply of ditto paper (today it would have been copier toner). Came the response: "But now, with all the volunteers, we've been able to give the pupils a chance for individual study exercises, so we've been running off ditto masters in larger numbers than ever before." So the principal wanted to advise his colleagues: "If you're going to start having volunteers, you'd better increase your paper supply requisition." What excellent, practical advice!

One way to estimate your costs for supplies might be to translate the cumulative number of hours served by volunteers (or anticipated to be served) annually into "full-time equivalent" (FTE) staff positions. For example, if an employee works 2,080 hours a year (40 hours per week x 52), then a volunteer program logging 10,000 hours of volunteer service per year can be said to give the organization the equivalent of 4.8 full-time employee hours of service, or 4.8 FTE. If you normally budget supplies using a formula of $xx per employee, to arrive at the supply budget for the volunteer program, simply take $xx and multiply it times the total of the number of paid staff in the volunteer program office *and* the FTE number of volunteers.[1]

Printing and Reproduction

This is a major line item for a volunteer program, especially in the first year. The following items all require printing or photocopying:

—volunteer application forms and other recordkeeping forms
—recruitment brochures, flyers, posters, mailings, and other tools

—recognition certificates, invitations, etc.
—possibly a volunteer newsletter (quarterly?)
—perhaps a volunteer handbook or manual (in the second year?)
—training materials

The amount necessary for postage   **Postage**
will depend, of course, on such
variables as whether the volunteer
program mails a volunteer newslet-
ter or intends to use mass mailings of any sort to recruit
volunteers.

The whole issue of insurance will   **Insurance**
be discussed later in this book.
Suffice it to say here that the cost
of accident and/or liability insur-
ance for volunteers may have to be a budget item if your existing agency insurance package does not already cover volunteers.
Supplementary automobile insurance may also be a need, if some
volunteers are utilized as drivers for your organization. Special,
one-time event insurance may also be necessary if the volunteers
run major fundraising extravaganzas for you.

First talk to your present insurance carrier, but be aware
that special programs designed specifically for coverage of volunteer insurance needs are available at reasonable cost. (See
Chapter 9 and Appendix B.)

Though it is optional to budget for   **Recognition**
a major volunteer recognition
event such as a party or a dinner,
some consideration should be
given to how the organization will say thank you to volunteers
(and perhaps also to the staff who supervise them). Certificates of
appreciation are not expensive, while gift items can be budgeted
at a wide range of cost. Even a minimal amount of money can
permit an enjoyable recognition event—punch and cookies can
show appreciation as well as a steak dinner can.

Enabling Funds   "Enabling" funds are reimburse-
                             ment given to volunteers for out-
                             of-pocket expenses incurred in the
                             course of volunteer service. This is
meant to "enable" people to give their services freely, especially
if the cost of volunteering would otherwise prohibit some people
from participating. The concept of enabling funds has grown in
acceptance in the field of volunteerism and stems from the desire
to diversify the corps of volunteers as much as possible. If consideration is not given to out-of-pocket costs, then too many programs will have as volunteers only those people who can afford
the "luxury" of volunteering. Older people on fixed incomes, students with little outside income, and low-income people will otherwise be shut out of the opportunity to give their time and energy to causes that they care about.

Some agencies are able to provide in-kind support of volunteers through existing resources, as opposed to having to budget funds to reimburse cash expenditures. Items offered by such
agencies include:

  —parking lot privileges or van transportation
  —meals on site
  —free uniforms or uniform cleaning services
  —refreshments, such as hot or cold drinks
  —access to an agency-run child care service

When an organization can indeed offer these types of items to
volunteers, they might be budgeted under the heading of "benefits" and certainly should be described as such in recruitment
materials.

If your agency does not have the option of offering such
benefits as in-kind, consider the types of items that cost volunteers money and therefore might be reimbursed by the organization, such as:

  —transportation to and from the assignment
  —child care costs
  —telephone or postage costs for work done at home
  —special clothing needs (uniforms, aprons, work gloves,
     etc.)
  —money spent directly on clients, such as taking a child to
     a movie or buying supplies for an art class

Some agencies offer reimbursement to volunteers on the basis of economic need. Clearly this is a tricky area and requires thoughtful procedures to encourage volunteers to identify their expenses. Philosophically, I believe in making reimbursement available to every volunteer and then allowing those who prefer to consider the money they spend as a donation to say so.

Volunteer expenses should be budgeted visibly to acknowledge their existence. If some (even most) volunteers select to donate these costs to the agency, this can be shown as "revenue" to offset the "expense" category (see Chapter 11). But for most volunteers, these out-of-pocket costs *are* a financial consideration and good management requires the recognition and reporting of such agency resources.

Travel

This line item covers the cost of public outreach and recruitment. The director of volunteers and other program representatives will be making speeches and presentations throughout the community and such travel or public transportation should be reimbursed.

Travel also should accommodate trips to state and national meetings or conferences by volunteer program staff and participants.

Professional Development

Professional development includes funds for memberships in various professional societies (see Appendix B on volunteerism resources) and registration fees for workshops and conferences, both for the volunteer office staff and for *key volunteers*. This is one way that an organization can build loyalty among volunteers: demonstrate interest in *their* professional development, too. It is perfectly all right to ask that a volunteer make a commitment of time for all funds expended on his/her training—just as you would negotiate with a salaried staff member for a commitment in return for tuition reimbursement. If the time commitment is not honored, then the person (employee or volunteer) would be expected to pay back the money extended.

Volunteerism journal subscriptions and book purchases for an in-house library also fall into the category of professional development.

Volunteer Training   Training expenses may include fees to speakers, film rentals, books and handout materials, etc. to support volunteer training programs.

Other   Every program will have some sort of special need unique to its setting. The point to be made, however, is that volunteer offices often have "odd" requisitions. Who else may ask for 300 balloons?! The creative aspects of recruitment, motivation and recognition require supplies that set a tone or atmosphere different from the rest of the facility. So be prepared for the unexpected!

A Note on   While we have been discussing the
Decentralizing   allocation of a budget directly to
Expenses   the volunteer program, under the administration of the director of volunteers, it is also legitimate to provide for some of the expenses of volunteers within the budget of each unit that will involve volunteer workers. This allows for categorical accounting and may give you a more realistic understanding of the true costs of volunteer participation.

Finding the Funds   One of the purposes of budgeting is to recognize the total cost of running a volunteer program. However, nothing says that all budget items must be paid for out of current organization monies. Quite a number of the items listed above can be covered by specific donations (both cash and in-kind) or by special fundraising events.

Remember that funds expended on volunteers are "leveraged" into more hours and types of service than the same amount of money could pay for in salaries. This multiplying factor can be a powerful argument to a corporate donor or a foundation grants officer, who might well consider funding support of volunteers in your organization.

The following pages contain a "Volunteer Program Budget Worksheet" arranged with the same categories and sequence as presented in this chapter. When a line ends with an "S," it indicates a start-up cost that does not repeat in subsequent years.

Worksheet

[1]G. Neil Karn, "The No-Apologies Budget," *Voluntary Action Leadership*, Spring 1984, pp. 29-31.

VOLUNTEER PROGRAM BUDGET WORKSHEET

PERSONNEL

Director of Volunteers $_____
    (Full-time or _____ hours per week)

Assistant Director of Volunteers   _____
    (Full-time or _____ hours per week)

Secretary   _____

Other assigned staff: _____
   _____

Benefits (estimated @ _____% of total salaries)   _____

(Estimate of cost of staff time to train
and supervise volunteers: $_____)

                         Sub-total—Personnel: $_____

OPERATIONAL COSTS

*Note that initial start-up costs are differentiated by an "S." Most of these items
are one-time expenditures, though several also involve additional purchases
each year as the volunteer program grows or to replenish inventory.*

Furniture and Equipment:

    Office furniture for the volunteer office,
    including desks, chairs, lamps, etc.   _____S

    File cabinets   _____S

    Computer(s)/typewriter(s)   _____S

    Volunteer recordkeeping software   _____S

    Other equipment:_____   _____S

Coat racks, storage cabinets, lounge
furniture, etc. for volunteers $_____S

Bulletin boards and exhibit equipment   _____S

Slide projector and screen   _____S

Sub-total—Furn./Equip.: $_____

Telephone:

Installation of instruments   _____S

Monthly service charge x 12   _____

Toll calls/long distance x 12   _____

Reimbursement to volunteers for calls made
at home on agency's behalf   _____

Sub-total—Telephone: _____

Supplies:

Office and maintenance supplies, estimated @
($____ per person per year) x (number of
volunteer program office employees + FTE
volunteer staff)   _____

Sub-total—Supplies: _____

Printing and Reproduction:

Photocopying ($____/mo. x 12)   _____

Printing of volunteer office forms   _____S

Printing of recruitment materials
(both initial and ongoing expense; some
quality pieces plus numerous offset or
photocopied flyers)

Printing of recognition event certificates,
program book, etc. $_____

Production of periodic volunteer office
newsletter   _____

Printing of volunteer program manual/
handbook   _____S

Other:_____   _____

*Note need to reprint inventory of some of the above
as an ongoing expense.*

                          Sub-total—Printing: $_____

Postage:

Regular correspondence, $____/mo. x 12   _____

Periodic mass mailings for recruitment   _____

Periodic bulk mailing of newsletter   _____

                          Sub-total—Postage: _____

Insurance:

(May be included in overall agency policy,
or a special rider, or a specific new policy.)   _____

                          Sub-total—Insurance: _____

Recognition:

(Depending on event, may include food costs,
entertainment, hall rental, gifts, pins, etc.)   _____

                          Sub-total—Recognition: _____

Enabling Funds:

      Reimbursement for volunteer mileage
      or transportation $_____

      Reimbursement to volunteers for out-of-pocket
      expenses incurred while serving clients
      (e.g., purchase of art supplies,
      taking a child to the zoo, etc.)   _____

      Purchase or loan of volunteer uniforms
      or special clothing   _____

      Other reimbursements: _____   _____

                         Sub-total—Enabling: $_____

Travel:

      Volunteer office staff local and intermediate
      distance travel for recruitment outreach   _____

      Travel to state or national conferences
      (for volunteer program staff and
      designated volunteers)   _____

                         Sub-total—Travel: _____

Professional Development:

      Registration fees for seminars, conferences, etc.
      (for volunteer program staff and
      designated volunteers)   _____

      Journal subscriptions, books, etc.   _____

      Membership fees for professional associations   _____

                         Sub-total—Prof. Dev.:   _____

Volunteer Training:

    Reproduction of handout materials or
    purchase of books for volunteers $_____

    Slides and training materials   _____

    Film/video rental or purchase fees   _____

    Speaker fees   _____

              Sub-total—Training: $_____

Other:_____   _____

              Sub-total—Other: _____

              TOTAL COSTS: $_____

ALLOCATION OF ORGANIZATIONAL RESOURCES

    Staff time

    Space

    Maintenance services

    Access to organizational equipment and supplies

    In-kind volunteer benefits, such as meals

STAFFING THE
VOLUNTEER PROGRAM

Decisions regarding the staffing of the volunteer program deserve careful consideration. How you go about designating or hiring the leadership of the program will be influenced by the goals you have for the utilization of volunteers. While it should be obvious that your staffing plan must fit the number and functions of volunteers you anticipate, it may not be obvious how to develop a "formula" to determine the right "fit."

Identifying a Leader

The vast majority of people who direct volunteer programs do not do so as a full-time job. Rather, they work part-time at volunteer management while actually primarily filling a different function in the organization; they have been asked to assume leadership of the volunteer program in addition to their other responsibilities. In many cases they were "anointed" into the leadership of volunteers; they did not seek the extra responsibility and felt they had little or no option when their administrator offered it to them. Additionally, they continue to view their original job description as their priority and try to "squeeze in" the volunteer program as a secondary set of tasks. In terms of career goals, most of these part-timers have no interest in pursuing the volunteer management field. They see themselves rather as "social workers," "park rangers," "occupational therapists," or "probation officers" and consider the volunteerism "piece" of their jobs as something they will escape when they move up.

Logically, someone who sees volunteer leadership as secondary (perhaps even as distracting) will rarely give the type of

direction to the program that will make it achieve its true potential. So why "anoint" a reluctant director of volunteers?

The first step is to decide whether or not you are able (or
willing) to create a new budget line for a volunteer program staff
member. Since the dollar value of volunteer services far exceeds
the actual funds expended (see Chapter 11), it may be worthwhile to wait in creating or expanding your volunteer component
until funds can be found. A special fundraising event or a special
grant request might create the first year's salary, especially if you
plan to begin with a part-time staff member. At least this part-
timer will devote *all* of his or her on-site time to the subject of
volunteers. And the time will be devoted willingly and enthusi-
astically because it will be this person's primary job responsibility. The difference in possible achievement of goals because of
this factor of *primary* responsibility cannot be overestimated and
outweighs even the time limitations of a shorter work schedule.

If a new budget line is absolutely not possible, then you
should begin by discovering who on staff might actually *want* to
learn about volunteer management. Even if the interested staff
member functions in a work area that seems tangential to what
you plan for volunteers, the factor of free choice should weigh
heavily in favor of giving that staff member the responsibility for
volunteers.

When I conduct workshops for people who are part-time
directors of volunteers in addition to carrying other agency job
responsibilities, I always ask whether they tried to clarify the following important points at the time they accepted their volunteer-
related tasks:

> —What exactly does "part time" mean? How many hours
> of the day or week will I be allowed to devote to vol-
> unteer management?

> —In what ways will my present workload be decreased in
> order to "make room" for my new volunteer program
> responsibilities?

> —At what level of program growth will my part-time status
> be reviewed to determine whether more time is needed
> for volunteer management or if the agency is ready for a
> full-time director of volunteers (not necessarily me)?

—What other agency resources will be made available to me in support of the new volunteer program?

—Does my immediate supervisor understand and completely accept the fact that my previous work patterns will now have to change, especially in terms of decreasing my former output in my primary area of service?

In all too many cases, these questions are not raised by either the new leader of volunteers or the CEO.[1] Because so many of these issues require decision-making authority, it would be helpful for the executive to consider these and other questions before selecting an existing staff member to take on the added responsibility of the volunteer program. Otherwise, volunteer management becomes nothing more than an addendum to an already busy schedule and, in fact, produces stress and tension among the staff as a whole.

It is probably just as pertinent to consider some of these issues even if a brand new employee will be hired to focus on leading the volunteer program as a sole responsibility, but on a part-time schedule. For example, at what point will you start thinking about increasing the number of work hours for the director of volunteers? Or, if you do not want to expand this position, at what level of growth will you consider the volunteer program "capped"?

Whether you delegate volunteer management to an existing staff member or hire a new part-time employee, also assign specific responsibilities for supporting the volunteer program to other agency staff. This makes it clear that volunteers will be part of everyone's job because they are now part of the organization's delivery of services. For example, the public relations staff should help with recruitment, the bookkeeper with recordkeeping, and the clerical pool with correspondence. It is up to you to distribute the work where it logically belongs and to specify the chain of command between the new head of the volunteer program and those other staff members working on behalf of the volunteer program.

Even when you are ready and able to designate a full-time director of volunteers, other organizational personnel will continue to have support roles to play in assuring that the volunteers become part of the team.

A Word on Titles   Questions may arise about what
                              job title to give the leader of your
                              volunteer program. More than
                              twenty years ago, Harriet Naylor
created a "career ladder" for volunteer administration within what
was then the U.S. Department of Health, Education and Welfare
which was subsequently picked up in the Department of Labor's
Dictionary of Occupational Titles. This may be useful, but do not
feel constrained by anything other than what truly matches your
situation. Naylor's ladder has three ascending levels:

> "Supervisor of Volunteers," who works directly with volun-
> teers but does not handle much decision-making about the
> program as a whole;

> "Coordinator of Volunteers," who is a manager, but not on
> the top level; and

> "Director of Volunteers," the top administrator of the vol-
> unteer program.

For our purposes in this book, I will use the term "Director of
Volunteers" as a sort of generic title—even though it is probably
more accurate to think of this position as coordinating or mobi-
lizing, rather than as directing. Another common title is "Director
of Volunteer Services," which properly emphasizes that activities,
not people, are being managed. Obviously, substitute whatever
title has been selected in your setting.

One more note. There is general agreement that the title
"Volunteer Director" is confusing to outsiders. It invariably raises the question: "Oh, you mean you are unsalaried, too?" Most
directors of volunteers prefer to avoid wasting time on explana-
tions and appreciate a more accurate title.

Since the first edition of this book, many changes have
occurred in the vocabulary of the volunteer world, particularly an
increasing withdrawal from the word "volunteer" itself. Today
students speak of doing "community service" or "service-learning," the court system applies "alternative sentencing," professional societies engage in *"pro bono publico"* projects. (See
Chapter 7 for a discussion of some of these new resources.) To
accommodate and welcome these diverse new sources of work-

ers who help without going on the payroll, a growing number of agencies are changing the name of their "Volunteer Office" to something like the Office of "Community Participation" or "Community Involvement." Then the title of the head of that program becomes "Director of Community Resources," for example.

If you are going to designate an existing staff member to be in charge of the volunteer program, consider adapting that person's job title to include indication of responsibility for volunteers, as well. First, this clarifies things for members of the public who will otherwise be contacted by a "Probation Officer" or a "Social Worker" with seemingly little connection to a volunteer program. Second, the title change tells the rest of staff that there has indeed been a change in that employee's function.

However, try to avoid sticking the phrase "and Volunteers" onto an existing title, such as the real-life example of "Coordinator of Beautification and Volunteers." This only tends to imply that volunteers are an afterthought. If necessary, allow the staff member to use two different job titles, separated as appropriate for different situations.

Defining the Job of Directing Volunteers

Appendix A provides a "Volunteer Management Task Outline" of the role of a director of volunteers. Katherine Noyes Campbell and I first published the full "Task Analysis" version of it in 1981 in *No Excuses: The Team Approach to Volunteer Management*, a book about part-time volunteer management, which we revised in 1995 as *The (Help!) I-Don't-Have-Enough-Time Guide to Volunteer Management*. We developed (and have continued to keep current) the complete "Volunteer Management Task Analysis" because we discovered that none of the major books or articles on volunteer administration actually offered a "job description" for a director of volunteers. The job functions were implied, perhaps, but nowhere were all the various elements of the job spelled out. Because you will be writing a job description for your volunteer leadership position, this appendix should be helpful.

In considering the necessary tasks of a director of volunteers, an unusual pattern emerges. The director of volunteers (whether part- or full-time) operates within a framework of activities that make this position substantially different from any other staff position—except, ironically, your own. It is useful to understand these differences because you will be able to help the program leader more effectively if you expect and approve these unique aspects of the work. Also, especially if you are re-defining an existing staff member's job to add volunteer management, you must recognize that these differences will affect that person's interrelationships with the rest of the staff.

Here are some of the job elements that make a director of volunteers unique in the organizational structure:

- The director of volunteers is one of the few members of the staff with responsibility both **inside and outside** the organization. S/he must have constant contact with the public, especially in order to recruit new volunteers. This contact is active, not passive—it requires outreach. But s/he is also involved on a daily basis with the work of the organization, since volunteers become unsalaried staff members and require his/her liaison supervision. This is really a very special consideration. The majority of staff have no ongoing "community" job functions; they work solely on client or in-house service provision. Staffers such as a director of public relations, on the other hand, have no actual responsibilities related to the delivery of client services. Usually only you, as executive director, combine both internal and external functions. You and the director of volunteers.

- Because of this public outreach, the director of volunteers' job requires **odd work hours**. Recruitment must accommodate itself to the availability of groups and applicants. This may mean evening screening interviews, weekend special events, breakfast speeches, or Saturday orientation sessions. Conversely, the director of volunteers will sometimes be out of the office during agency working hours, giving presentations or attending meetings. These work habits can be misunderstood by other staff if these special job responsibilities of the volunteer program are not explained. Also, burnout is a danger if the director of volunteers is not given flexibility in adapting her/his schedule to such odd hours.

Some directors of volunteers are caught in a double bind when they work in settings that do not permit "administrators" to earn compensatory time. The reasoning is that the demands of top level management require extra effort occasionally and that this periodic overtime is part of the job already recognized by the higher salary. This rationale is not applicable to the job of the director of volunteers. S/he will continuously have odd-hour commitments and should be able to adjust his/her 35 or 40 hours (or 20, etc.) per week to fit that week's schedule. If a particular period requires an unusual amount of evening or weekend activity, plus daytime responsibilities, the director of volunteers should be able to accrue compensatory time.

- The in-house side of the director of volunteers' job requires that s/he be aware of the **entire organization**. Since volunteers could be assigned to any unit or staff member, the head of the volunteer program is not "snooping" when s/he asks about the work load of any area of the agency. From the offices of senior management to the maintenance department, the director of volunteers must be alert to new needs for assistance. Who else but you shares this mandate?

    Having to be informed about so many different types of services also forces the director of volunteers to speak many "languages"—requests for volunteers will be submitted in the jargon of each department.

- In keeping with the comprehensive overview just described, the director of volunteers must deal with **staff at all levels** in order to determine volunteer assignments and provide liaison supervision. However, s/he is a *department head*. In day-to-day operations, this can produce confusion or suspicion: why is this department head talking to me about my job? Or: why is this department head talking to one of my people about the work done in this department? Even if all volunteer job descriptions are developed through the channel of the different department heads, once volunteers are assigned, the director of volunteers will be in touch with the actual supervisors, the line staff. This all makes the director of volunteers potentially threatening or, on the other hand, can undermine his/her status as a department head.

- While the volunteer department appears on paper (on the payroll, at least) as the smallest unit in the facility, the director of volunteers may actually **supervise more people** than any other administrator except the CEO— and perhaps even more than the CEO! This fact cannot be dismissed by such statements as: "yes, but those people are all part-time." Even if the hours given by the volunteers are not equivalent to the hours of service of full-time staff (and they well might be), the director of volunteers still has to interview every applicant, keep records on, orient and place every volunteer, etc. Here is one area in which "body count" does matter. The director of volunteers must know and relate to every volunteer in the program. Remember that each volunteer is a public relations agent for the organization, so the need to have some personal involvement with all volunteers is not unimportant. It is easy to overlook the cumulative effect of the numbers of volunteers who come through the volunteer office in any given period because no one ever sees all the volunteers in the same place at the same time. (Even recognition events usually bring out only a percentage of all volunteers who have been involved in a year.)

- A corollary of being responsible for so many people is that no one else **coordinates** a staff with so many different schedules and so many different backgrounds. The director of volunteers must work with volunteers of all ages (possibly from children to senior citizens), of varying educational levels, and perhaps with physical disabilities. Now add to this mixture the fact that volunteers select their own working schedules and you end up with something of a circus—with the director of volunteers as juggler! Some volunteers may work on a very exact, weekly schedule; others on an as-needed basis. Some come in every Monday and Wednesday morning, some all day Thursday, some every other Friday lunch-time, and some when the moon is full! The director of volunteers can never "call a staff meeting," yet is expected to organize the work of all these volunteers.

Another dimension of this factor is that the director of volunteers ends up working in a "fishbowl" environment. Because volunteers arrive and depart at different times of the day, the director of volunteers is continually interrupted—legitimately—by the need to touch bases with the volunteer workers.

- Rarely does anyone else in an organization know how volunteers are recruited and managed. The director of volunteers is the **"in-house expert"** on volunteers and, in this capacity, acts as their advocate. This includes having to educate other staff about the ways to support volunteers and pointing out inappropriate requests for volunteer services. Volunteer management is such a new profession that the director of volunteers may feel isolated, while other staff may have colleagues in the same profession right there in the agency.

- The director of volunteers has a **triple constituency** while everyone else in the organization has only two. Everyone—including the director of volunteers and the volunteers themselves—must be concerned about the needs of the clients/consumers/patients. All activities must be weighed in terms of whether the best service will be provided to this public. Second, everyone must be supportive of the organization itself. This means that each person must uphold the policies of the agency and must work to achieve its mission. In fact, when an employee (or volunteer) can no longer support the organization's mission or policies, it is time to leave the job.

  However, the director of volunteers has a third obligation: to represent the *volunteer perspective*. This point of view may sometimes be in conflict with the first two constituents and may, in practice, cause occasional tension between the director of volunteers and others in the organization. This is appropriate and the CEO should recognize that the director of volunteers is doing his/her job well when the volunteer perspective is expressed. It might help to recognize that the director of volunteers *facilitates* the involvement of volunteers...s/he does not "control" volunteers.

- The director of volunteers is the only person who has the **mandate to dream** about new projects without immediately having to limit such inspiration with the thought, "how will we pay for this?" Though volunteers are not free, they can test new ideas initially without much cash flow. This is a very special role for the volunteer office.

Given these things that make the director of volunteers different from other staff, you might consider how s/he can be of direct support to you as CEO. For example, are you involving the director of volunteers in your strategies for good public relations? Are you sharing long-range planning ideas with him or her so that volunteers can be integrated into planning from the very beginning? Do you ask for advice in working with volunteer board members? Are you utilizing the director of volunteers' across-departments staff contacts to give you insight into the operations of the agency?

Qualifications for Being a Director of Volunteers

The field of volunteer administration is still developing as a profession. While you should seek someone to be your director of volunteers who has experience in the field, you may have to select someone with potential to learn the job. The following are some qualifications you might seek:

—Ability to articulate a positive point of view about volunteers: why they are important; what their potential might be in your setting; etc. This is a vital area. You don't want to hire someone with negative stereotypes about volunteers. How can s/he then help the rest of staff to work successfully with volunteers? Also, the self-fulfilling prophecy syndrome means that if the person is not positive about volunteers, s/he will never run a creative, energetic program.

—Vision—both of what volunteers can accomplish and of where your agency might go in the future.

—Understanding of the expanding scope of the field of volunteerism, including the many types of community resources that have emerged in the last decade that may use different terminology for their community service.

—Strong management skills.

—Strong interpersonal skills. An effective director of volunteers has warmth and a degree of charisma. Potential volunteers are encouraged to join your organization through the image portrayed by the director of volunteers, their first contact with you. S/he must be able to convey friendliness and efficiency, and must also be able to get to know each recruit well enough to make appropriate assignments.

—Enthusiasm and energy. The director of volunteers creates an atmosphere for the volunteer program and it must be a lively one.

—Comfortable presentation style and public speaking ability. Remember that the demands of recruitment and training will put this person in the public eye and in front of groups often.

—Familiarity with community resources.

—Skill in task analysis, since work must be divided into manageable parts that can be assigned to volunteers giving a few hours at a time.

—Ability to handle/juggle details, especially the demands of scheduling and task delegation.

—Willingness to adapt good ideas from other settings to the special needs of your facility.

It is imperative that your director of volunteers be a good administrator. But it is *equally* imperative that s/he have the personality needed to be a *leader*. Since volunteers are not rewarded by a paycheck, the director of volunteers must have the ability to motivate people and to maintain high morale among volunteers (and salaried staff).

When you interview candidates for the job of director of volunteers, you might ask yourself whether you will feel comfortable in working with this applicant personally. As we have been discussing, the director of volunteers is in a position of genuine importance to you as the top executive. S/he should be an assistant to you in planning and implementing new projects. Also, s/he will be a representative of your agency in the community.

It is helpful to ask job applicants what volunteering they themselves have done in the past or are doing now. The way they answer this question—tone and enthusiasm as well as concrete details—should be a clue to their attitude about volunteerism. However, be careful not to fall into the trap of assuming that, just because a person has done *volunteering* personally, s/he is automatically able to *direct* a volunteer program. This line of reasoning is just as faulty as implying that any employee of an agency can also run that agency! Experience as a volunteer is useful background for understanding the value and potential of volunteers, but the skills of recruitment, supervision, or recordkeeping are generally not gained by being a line volunteer handling specific client-related tasks.

On the other hand, if the person has been a volunteer administrative assistant in another volunteer program office, or has been an *officer* of an all-volunteer organization, or a coordinator of a fundraising event, then you may be correct to assume those experiences would translate well into the management responsibilities of your volunteer program.

How to Find a Director of Volunteers

Increasingly, it is possible to find people with experience in volunteer administration. It is more important to seek someone who has demonstrated ability to mobilize volunteers in any setting, than to insist upon finding someone with a complete understanding of your type of facility. The setting can be learned more easily than the techniques of volunteer management. Also, you have lots of in-house resources to train the person about your setting. Who on staff can train the person in volunteerism?

If you accept the fact that volunteer administration is a generic profession, this opens the door to many recruitment possibilities. You might send a job opening announcement to any of the following resources (described at greater length in Appendix B), if they operate in your community:

> —the local Volunteer Center
> —the State Office of Volunteerism or Commission on Citizen Service
> —the local "DOVIA" (Directors of Volunteers in Agencies) association
> —the regional officers of the Association for Volunteer Administration

Think about which facilities have large volunteer programs. If they are large enough to have several salaried staff members, there might be someone presently in an assistant position who is ready to move up into a full directorship. This might also be true of some administrative volunteers who have been, in essence, apprenticing as leaders of other volunteers. So it is worth sending a notice to such settings.

The skills of directing volunteers can be learned in non-agency environments, too. For example, anyone with background in organizing successful political campaigns (either for partisan candidates or for non-partisan issues) knows a great deal about volunteers. So do special event organizers, alumni association staff, and many fire chiefs. Former presidents of large, all-volunteer organizations also have experience in the nuances of organizing voluntary workers.

As time goes on, you may become aware of a growing number of people who have the credential of "CVA"—"Certified in Volunteer Administration." The CVA designation is awarded by the Association for Volunteer Administration, the field's international professional society. It is given after an applicant has completed a rather extensive certification process, including the development of a portfolio documenting performance-based competencies. The process includes peer review and has a built-in continuing education requirement. Applicants must have at least two year's experience in volunteer administration before they may begin the certification process.

If you interview someone with the CVA designation, you can be assured that s/he has demonstrated a commitment to volunteer management as a profession and a career. You can also be comfortable about the person's basic understanding of the role of a director of volunteers. Beyond that, you must determine for yourself whether the person fits into your facility and can handle the special demands of leading volunteers in your setting.

Note that the CVA is not the same as a "certificate" from an academic institution awarded at the completion of a certain number of courses or non-credit workshops. Such certificate programs are underway in a number of states and represent an important trend in training for volunteer managers.

Many people fall into the field of volunteer administration unintentionally. (I did!) Because it is not yet widely possible to prepare for this profession through formal academic schooling, you will find that directors of volunteers come from a wide variety of backgrounds. On-the-job experience is what counts in most cases, though some applicants will also be able to document having attended single courses or continuing education workshops on various topics in volunteer management. In fact, if someone lists previous job experience in volunteerism, you should specifically ask what educational experiences s/he made use of. Has s/he ever attended a volunteerism conference locally, on the state level, or nationally? Does s/he subscribe to any of the journals in the field? These types of questions should quickly indicate whether the person has indeed connected her/himself to the "field" of volunteerism, beyond the daily tasks of the job.

Some people will apply for the job because they see it as a steppingstone into your type of setting. They are not necessarily interested in running a volunteer program, but rather want to do any job that will get them in the door. This motivation is not self-evidently bad, but it should be approached cautiously. Will this person devote him/herself to the needs of the volunteer program while s/he fills this position? Or will s/he look for the quickest way to move into another slot? The applicant must be open to the possibility that s/he will enjoy the position of director of volunteers enough to end up sticking with it and taking it to its maximum potential. You do not need a reluctant director of volunteers.

One reason why some people resist taking a job as director of volunteers is the mistaken impression that it is a field without a career "ladder." Because it is isolated in most settings from the other staff positions, there seems to be no clear way for a competent director of volunteers to move up. The real career mobility in volunteerism is to seek higher administrative responsibility (your job!). The director of volunteers is already in the perfect spot for learning a great deal about overall agency functioning. S/he will be involved in planning and implementation of a wide array of agency projects. If s/he is promoted into a Vice-Presidency or an Assistant Directorship, overall responsibility for the volunteer program can remain with that person—only s/he will now supervise the new director of volunteers. Directors of volunteers are actually in training to become CEOs—and when they reach that career point, they should be as supportive of the volunteer program staff as they always wanted their former bosses to be!

Secretarial Assistance

From the very beginning, a volunteer program needs the help of a secretary. This is as crucial to a part-time director as to a full-time one. If you have designated an existing employee as leader of volunteers, be sure also to designate consistent, available clerical support.

Recruitment campaigns, records on a growing corps of volunteers, preparation for such things as orientation or training sessions, recognition events—all demand a great deal of clerical activity. The program secretary also provides important office coverage while the director of volunteers is out in the community or busy elsewhere in the facility. Such coverage is vital because prospective applicants and active volunteers deserve to be able to make contact with someone who is knowledgeable about the volunteer program. Also, many secretaries actually supervise the work of volunteers assigned to tasks under the jurisdiction of the volunteer office.

One frustration often expressed by directors of volunteers is that their requests for a program secretary are met with the rather smug response: "why don't you get a volunteer to do it?" There is no doubt in the world that it would be possible to recruit volunteers capable of handling the secretarial tasks of the volunteer office. The problem is one of schedule. One of the main purposes of a salary is to be able to "demand" a predetermined work schedule. If the director of volunteers has to rely on volunteers for necessary clerical work, then s/he may have to recruit as many as eight or ten volunteers to fill all the necessary hours of service. This creates a situation in which the services of volunteers "cost" the director of volunteers much supervision and coordination time—at the expense of other necessary work. A paid secretary is a vital link in the program's operation. Volunteers can handle a great deal of the program's clerical tasks, but not those that need daily, timely attention with consistency and continuity.

Volunteers in Charge?

In somewhat the same vein, executives tend to ask if it is possible to operate a volunteer program with a *volunteer* as the head. There is no uniformly right answer to this question. It really depends upon whether or not you have a willing volunteer with both the capability and the schedule necessary to be the director of volunteers. Finding the capability is not the hard part; getting a long-term, multi-hour per week commitment is. If you are lucky enough to have someone available and willing to be a staff member at no salary, by all means accept his or her services. But recognize that you are not necessarily building for the future if you do not *budget* for an employee. It is better to create a staff position and indicate willingness to pay a salary, and then work with a volunteer for as long as that person can stay with you. In this way, if the volunteer leader has to resign, you are not caught completely unprepared to replace him or her. Volunteers able to give the necessary hours to head a volunteer program are few and far between. And if you end up recruiting, say, five volunteers to share the job—are *you* going to supervise and coordinate them?!

Many salaried directors of volunteers have indeed discovered that volunteers make excellent mid-level supervisors of other volunteers—sort of a team approach to running the office. Such administrative volunteers can be project coordinators for specific activities, orient groups of new volunteers, or follow-up on work being done by other volunteers off-site. This is one way that a director of volunteers is able to manage a growing program. It is a legitimate utilization of volunteers because it can offer flexible scheduling in reasonable chunks of time. However, even a program with several such administrative volunteers will eventually require a paid assistant director of volunteers, because the supervision demands of the administrative volunteers can also grow beyond what one employee can adequately give.

Graduate students majoring in some aspect of organizational management may be an excellent source of help in the early stages of a volunteer program or the piloting of a new volunteer project. If it is possible to develop a nine-month internship of two days per week and focus it entirely on volunteer program development, your organization may have found a cost-effective and reasonable way to get started. Full-time stipended programs such as VISTA or AmeriCorps (both in transition as this revised edition goes to press) frequently encourage placements that involve community resource mobilization. But do not forget that students or young adults are frequently inexperienced in the practical issues of management. Volunteer administration, as we have been discussing, is a rather sophisticated area that deserves the attention of a skilled manager.

Also, be certain to designate a supervisor who can genuinely help the student and who can carry on after the student leaves. In fact, it is important to plan ahead for the transition of leadership when the internship is over, because you do not want a gap in administration over the summer months or longer.

The danger of utilizing a graduate student is that the volunteer program may therefore be viewed as "low level," since the intern will hardly have real authority with which to make decisions or set standards. So your executive involvement in enforcing commitment to volunteers will be imperative.

If the volunteer program will be or is headed by a volunteer or a committee of volunteers, be alert to the possible ways conflict might develop between these leaders and the salaried staff—and do not unwittingly add to it yourself! The biggest problem is that the person may not be treated as a genuine administrator and will constantly be justifying her or his authority. Clearly, you will set the tone for the rest of the staff by the way you "model" acceptance of this volunteer.

Include the person, by name, on your department head memos. Invite the volunteer to staff meetings and give her or him time on the agenda as any other department head. Expect the same reports and other accountability from the unsalaried director of volunteers as you would from any other staff member. Supply the volunteer with an office, a telephone extension, and business cards paid for by the agency. All of these things demonstrate that the volunteer has been accepted by you as the leader of the volunteer program. Another important way to indicate that the volunteer is a part of staff is to show the program budget over which the volunteer department head has jurisdiction.

Other Staffing Needs

As mentioned in the rationale for a program secretary, the volunteer office has some special considerations in terms of coverage. Certainly every unit of the organization wants to be accessible to the public and therefore makes provisions for such things as telephone coverage when all staff are away from their desks. But for the volunteer program, this need is more than just for message taking. The hardest step in applying for a volunteer position is to make the initial telephone call. Therefore the attitude and tone of the person answering the phone on behalf of the volunteer program is critical. If the prospective volunteer hears disinterest or even discourtesy, the whole recruitment effort may be aborted. In fact, the agency representative should be saying things like: "We're so glad you called and I know that our director of volunteers will be delighted to call you back." This simply is not the way most staff "take messages" for each other!

As CEO, you can make certain that employees are trained to support the volunteer office in its relations with the public. Telephone switchboard operators, reception desk personnel and others with "frontline" public contact responsibilities should project a friendly and appreciative image to all prospective and active volunteers. In a small office, this requirement extends to all staff who routinely answer phones or greet visitors for one another. (This is a great example of behavior change that benefits everyone, not just volunteers!)

Unfortunately, since the first edition of this book, we have all grown accustomed to the ubiquitous presence of automated voice mail systems. It is my personal hope that by the time a third edition rolls around, we will have learned our lesson! Many organizations need to evaluate the cost of replacing a live voice on the telephone with a computer. It certainly projects an impersonal image to clients and the community, especially if people are calling when in distress. For prospective volunteers, voice mail may be an unhelpful hurdle to jump in the process of considering whether or not to give time. At a minimum, test the system to make sure that contact with the volunteer office is a specific option to select and that it is easy to leave a message. Not to mention assuring that a staff member calls back soon!

One other staffing point is that the director of volunteers is not a substitute for volunteers. If a scheduled volunteer is absent for whatever reason, it is not appropriate to expect the director of volunteers to come to the unit and handle the volunteer's work for that day. This is, of course, no different from expectations we hold for employee supervisors. If an employee is not present, the work is generally held until the person returns; the supervisor does not step in to do it unless some emergency warrants it. Actually, since volunteers are deployed in the facility in various work areas, if a task assigned to an absent volunteer is critical, the most appropriate "substitute" would be a line worker in that unit—not the director of volunteers who is not part of that unit.

Volunteer Program Advisory Committee

Both for purposes of planning and evaluation, it might be helpful to develop an advisory committee for the volunteer program. Such a committee need not be large nor need it meet frequently. But it should be representative of management, line employees and volunteers themselves. When appropriate, recipients of service should also be included.

Because the director of volunteers must have a comprehensive overview of the whole organization, this committee can work to insure that all points of view are considered when new projects are begun. The committee therefore supports the director of volunteers by channeling information to the volunteer program and also by explaining program activities to others throughout the organization. This is an excellent way to prevent some of the possible tension between volunteers and salaried staff.

Enlarging the Volunteer Management Staff

Apart from the job description and schedule of the leader of the volunteer program, at some point you will probably need to make decisions about when the program will require a full-time position, when to add one or more assistant directors of volunteers, and when to add one or more program secretaries.

It is difficult to give absolute guidelines for determining the right staffing pattern. However, the following criteria should be part of any discussion of personnel assessment:

> —Are volunteers going to be active evenings, weekends, or during hours beyond a "regular" work week? The answer to this question might immediately suggest the need for an evening volunteer supervisor, for example, or might help to determine the regular schedule of the full-time director of volunteers (11 a.m. to 7 p.m., for example, or Tuesday through Saturday).

> —What is the maximum number of employees that a supervisor is normally asked to supervise?

Some management books feel that no one should be expected to productively supervise more than five full-time people. Whatever your cut-off point in terms of employee management, apply it to the volunteer program.

First, what is the FTE ("full-time equivalent," as we discussed in the section on budgeting for supplies) of the volunteers working *directly* under the supervision of the director of volunteers? This might include volunteer positions such as clerical assistants, in-service trainers, volunteer office librarians, record-keepers, etc. The assessment of how many FTE volunteer staff are being supervised is especially pertinent if the volunteer office directly coordinates certain volunteer projects, such as an annual fundraising event or a daily meal delivery program.

Second, what is the FTE of the volunteers for whom the volunteer office is *indirectly* responsible (but still maintains records, handles recognition, etc.)?

How large would you allow your organization's salaried staff to become without adding to the number of employees in, say, the personnel office? The main point is to apply the same standards to the volunteer office and be sure that adequate staff is available to provide the best management of the program. Keep in mind that one way you demonstrate your organization's commitment to volunteers is how you designate and then support the volunteer program's leadership.

[1]For a more in-depth discussion of laying the groundwork for a part-time director of volunteers, see *The (Help!) I-Don't-Have-Enough-Time Guide to Volunteer Management*, by   Katherine Noyes Campbell and Susan J. Ellis, Energize, 1995.

UNDERSTANDING THE VOLUNTEER/EMPLOYEE RELATIONSHIP

It may be surprising to learn that the single most requested training topic in volunteer management is not how to recruit volunteers—rather, it is how to develop good volunteer/salaried staff relationships. Regardless of setting, age or size of program, everyone wants to know how to build an effective team between volunteers and employees. Why is this so hard? Is there something inevitable about tension between these two sets of workers?

One thing is certain. If the subject of volunteer/employee relationships is ignored as a management issue, each employee (and volunteer) will develop his or her own way of interacting. Such diverse standards will indeed produce confusion if not outright hostility. The main purpose of this chapter, therefore, is to emphasize the need for the *involvement of top administration in setting the tone and policy for effective integration of volunteers into the organization.* This cannot be left in the hands of the director of volunteers. S/he does not have the authority to make rules for the whole organization or to enforce such rules. As the nonsalaried personnel of the organization, volunteers deserve direct attention from the executive level.

To assess whether your agency has planned sufficiently for good volunteer/salaried staff relationships, consider the following questions:

—What happens (in terms of actual procedures) when a volunteer makes a mistake or does something wrong?

—If a dispute develops between a volunteer and an employee, is the employee always presumed to be right? Is the employee presumed to have more rights?

—Are there clearly defined channels for volunteers to make suggestions, voice criticisms, etc.?

—How many members of the salaried staff have ever had formal training (not just on-the-job experience) in how to supervise volunteers?

—Has any member of staff recently refused to work with volunteers (this means refusing to develop a job description for possible volunteer assistance—not turning down a specific applicant who was not appropriate)? Why? Did anyone question that staff member on his/her refusal?

—Has any employee ever been evaluated on his/her level of competence in supervising volunteers?

—When was the last time an employee was given any tangible recognition for working successfully with volunteers?

—Is it common practice to refer to the "professional" staff versus the "volunteers"?

—Do all labor contracts (if you have one or more employee unions) include clarification of the role of volunteers in the agency and, especially, their role in time of a possible strike?

—How many volunteers have left the agency in the past year due to dissatisfaction with their acceptance level in the organization?

If you answered these questions honestly (and no one will ever know, so go ahead!), you might find yourself saying "I'm not really sure." *That's* "benign neglect." If all these questions were reversed and asked about salaried staff, you'd feel responsible as a manager to know the answers. Volunteers tend to be invisible workers.

These questions hint at some of the key volunteer/salaried staff relationship areas requiring policy formation and top administrative involvement.

One situation crops up so frequently that it is often not even
perceived as a problem at all: the
premise that an employee has the
choice of whether or not to work with volunteers. In many ways,
this is the crux of the entire problem and so deserves scrutiny.

Danger Signs:
Refusal to Accept
Volunteers

In most organizations, the director of volunteers recruits
volunteers and, after screening applicants, matching them to the
most appropriate jobs, and orienting them, assigns them to the
day-to-day supervision of paid staff. Some volunteers do work
under the direct supervision of the volunteer office, but the
majority are "deployed" throughout the organization in a decen-
tralized approach to volunteer management. The premise is that
line staff are the ones most knowledgeable about the tasks to be
done and therefore should work directly with volunteers in
accomplishing those tasks.

If you are going to institute a volunteer program or
strengthen the one you already have, you must deal with the
question: do we, as an organization, believe *qualified* volunteers
are vital enough to integrate them everywhere? Please note the
word "qualified." In every instance, this book advocates the
appropriate placement of volunteers who either were recruited
for special skills or were given training by the agency to fill necessary positions.

Some of the resistance to working with volunteers comes
from stereotypes about what volunteers are like. Employees
should never be asked to work with uncommitted, unqualified,
or unpleasant people—whether unsalaried or salaried! But if we
start with the supposition that the volunteer program will be managed well and that all volunteers will be recruited to match the
requirements of available assignments, then prejudices about volunteers should be dispelled.

As long as employees are given the choice or act as though
they have the choice of accepting volunteers as co-workers, top
administration is sending mixed messages about volunteers. The
implication is that working with volunteers is in some way "additional" to the primary work to be done. Despite the fact that the
organization has established a "volunteer program" and allocated
resources to it, utilization of volunteers is viewed as an option

that any individual staff member is free to accept or reject. When no negative reaction follows from an employee's decision not to work with volunteers and, further, when the employee who does work with volunteers receives no positive reinforcement, the only logical conclusion is: *it does not matter to administration.* Volunteers are "nice" and maybe even "helpful," but they are certainly not *essential.*

Think what would happen if, using a hospital as an example, a nurse unilaterally decided s/he would not work with the physical therapists. Whenever the PTs come around, s/he politely refuses to work cooperatively. Such behavior sounds so absurd it is even hard to take the example seriously. Yet, in hospital after hospital around the country, the Volunteer Services Department has had to accept rejection from nurses and other medical staff who simply—with no reasons given or required—opt not to "take" a volunteer. (Feel free to substitute any other kind of agency setting.)

In most organizations right now, the director of volunteers is placed in the position of going around to the salaried staff and asking: "do you want a volunteer?" The tone is one of, can we do each other a favor? How ridiculous. If the organization has seen fit to establish and fund a volunteer component, then it is a part of the agency. All employees must collaborate with that unit in exactly the same way they are expected to work with the physical therapists, the clerical pool, the maintenance staff, or the public relations department.

The director of volunteers must be held accountable to find and prepare the best possible volunteers. If s/he cannot do this, it is grounds for dismissal. But if the director of volunteers is indeed fulfilling this responsibility, then no other staff member has the right to judge the volunteer program negatively—and therefore must cooperate. If an employee is uncomfortable with volunteers, the proper administrative response should be to *offer training*, not to permit him or her to avoid this aspect of the job.

Ironically, some directors of volunteers have contributed to the perpetuation of this cycle of "acceptance of rejection." They do not confront the resistant employee on the grounds that they prefer not placing volunteers into a negative supervisory situation. So, out of reasonable concern for the morale and motivation of the volunteers, the director protectively ignores the staff member who refuses to work with volunteers. While this may be proper management in the case of a particular volunteer ready to work immediately, it is poor long-range planning. The director of volunteers must identify resistant staff members and—with the help of the chief executive—change their behavior.

Even if the salaried staff under-stand the value of volunteer involvement to the agency and its clients, in day-to-day operations

What Causes Tension

the interface between the two sets of workers can be difficult. Both the perspective of the employee and the volunteer must be understood in order to analyze what causes tension between volunteers and salaried staff. Specifically, it is necessary to identify:

—the perceived threats posed by volunteers to salaried staff; and,

—the reasons volunteers may be resistant to supervision by salaried staff.

Because this is first and foremost a human relations situation, it is helpful to remember that the dynamics involved do not always relate to real issues but reflect fear, misunderstanding, and prejudice—on both sides. So in order to prevent or solve interrelationship problems, it is necessary to consider the possible factors involved.

Here are just some of the real or imagined threats volunteers pose to employees. This list is not meant to imply that every staff member

Threats to the Salaried Staff

harbors these fears, but to show that there is a wide range of possible reactions to the offer of volunteer assistance. Recognize that few people will ever actually voice these thoughts out loud since, in principle, it seems ungrateful to complain about "free help." It is also possible for staff members to acknowledge the importance of volunteers to the agency at large without necessarily being happy about being asked to work directly with a volunteer in their own unit.

Please note that some of the following issues are not mythical. If the staff feels that administration does not realize some of the possible problems volunteers create, they will be reluctant to tell you their genuine reactions to the idea of volunteers—instead, they will undercut (even sabotage) the program by refusing to be given a volunteer or by providing insufficient supervision to volunteers already on board.

—Volunteers will take paid jobs...maybe my job. *Here is a good example of just because you're paranoid, it does not mean someone is not out to get you! Is it really strange that, in today's economy, staff are fearful for their jobs? And have you ever discussed volunteers as budget "savers" rather than as budget "extenders"?*

—Volunteers will do a bad job and I'll be left with the blame, or the responsibility to "clean up." (And they can't be fired.)

—Volunteers will do a great job and I'll look less effective. *(Return to threat #1. . . will a great volunteer replace me? In fact, what do you think is most threatening? A volunteer who fails or one who succeeds? Because of uncertainty about the true agenda behind the involvement of volunteers, the most effective volunteer programs are frequently the ones with the biggest staff acceptance problems.)*

—Volunteers are spies. (To whom are they related? To whom do they talk after work? Are they watching the way I perform?) *The reality is that volunteers do indeed see the work being done—and not being done. If an employee is insecure about his or her performance, the thought of a volunteer uncovering weakness is scary.*

—Volunteers are amateurs. They do not know much and I'll have to train them from scratch, which takes a lot of time.

—Volunteers are highly trained and they do not want to be oriented to do it our (my) way. They can't be controlled.

—Volunteers are different from me. They are *(select any that apply)* younger, older, less educated, more educated, a different race or religion, from a different social or economic class, more or less knowledgeable about this community, etc.

—Volunteers gossip. They do not understand confidentiality.

—If these volunteers were really good workers, they'd all have paying jobs. (You mean a lot of them already do? Then how come they're also volunteering?)

—I do not know how to break my work into smaller tasks that can be delegated to a volunteer. I am also not sure that the time it would take me to do this would be won back in any savings by having the volunteer help me. Besides, I'd really rather do it myself so I can be certain it will be done right.

—I never learned about volunteer management in my formal education, so I'm not sure how to work with volunteers. But, because I take pride in being a "professional," how can I admit that I don't know how to work with volunteers?

—Volunteers want to spend too much time socializing with me.

—We have so little work space. I don't have the room to work with a volunteer.

—Volunteers are not dependable.

—You can't criticize a volunteer, so how can you make sure the work is done right?

—The client may like the volunteer better than me.

—All the things I can think of for a volunteer to do are the fun parts of my job. I don't want to give those up.

—I am jealous (though I'd never show it) that volunteers get all those thank-you's, special luncheons, and balloons. And they also get to choose their schedules and their work assignments. They even get to say "no" once in a while.

—My supervisor doesn't understand that working with volunteers takes some of my time.

—When I accepted this job, no one ever told me I was supposed to work with volunteers.

—There are no rewards for working well with volunteers.

—Why should I work with a volunteer? Volunteers "belong" to the director of volunteers and why should I do him/her the favor of supervising a volunteer?

—I am so new at my job that it is hard for me to explain parts of it to a volunteer.

—Volunteers only see a small part of the picture because they come in irregularly. Therefore their opinions and suggestions are not worth as much as mine because I understand the whole situation.

—If we act on all these new ideas, things will change around here.

—Do I have to say thank you all the time—even if I don't mean it?

—Volunteers interrupt my day/week.

In examining the range of these statements, it is obvious that even the best salaried staff members may be concerned about some of these issues. And in all honesty, their concern may be appropriate, especially if the organization has never clarified its policies about volunteers.

There are indeed practical issues involved in accommodating volunteers which employees should be encouraged to identify and discuss. These include such things as: volunteers *do* require staff time; volunteers *do* have more options for saying no; some volunteers *are* on board in order to learn new skills and therefore need extra attention in training.

Another factor is the diversity of your volunteer corps. Some volunteers will be recruited as highly-trained specialists, while others may come to your organization as trainees or to fill generalist roles such as friendly visiting. Unfortunately, this diversity sometimes results in volunteers being judged by the lowest common denominator. For example, because one unit utilizes high school students as volunteers, staff in another unit may be skeptical about the qualifications of volunteers who may be referred to them—they simply have trouble visualizing more skilled voluntary assistance.

Certain employees may have more justification than others for questioning the value to them of working with volunteers. Brand new **Special Cases**
staff members, for example, are so busy learning the ropes of their job that they really cannot yet delegate parts of it to someone else.

Some jobs or professions are not "people oriented" in that they involve limited contact with the public and the type of person entering them may prefer it that way. These jobs range from library book acquisitioner to zoo keeper to chef. At the very least, such staff members are inexperienced in supervising other people and may resent having this responsibility foisted on them "after the fact" of accepting a job description without mention of volunteers.

Finally there is the growing number of paraprofessional positions. Paraprofessionals are usually low on the "pecking order" of an organization anyway. They are directly threatened by the influx of volunteers because many of the things assigned to volunteers are related to the assistant work performed by paraprofessionals—and so job security is an honest issue. Negative attitudes by paraprofessionals about volunteers are compounded by the fact that often it is the paraprofessional who is assigned to supervise the volunteers—and very few paraprofessionals have the training, the time, or even the skill to do this adequately. If you have a paraprofessional level of staff, be alert to the possibility of misunderstanding of roles between them and some volunteers.

Volunteer
Resistance

It takes two to tango. Though the majority of problems between volunteers and employees stem from employee actions, in all fairness, volunteers also contribute to the hostilities. Never assume that volunteers are knowledgeable about volunteering. They bring the same stereotypes and prejudices to the situation as do employees. Also, volunteers rarely see the big agency picture since they are focused on the specific work they came to do.

Volunteers' real or imagined reasons for resistance to working effectively with paid staff may include:

—I am more qualified than the salaried staff, so why should I let them boss me around?

—I am here to help out and the staff should be grateful. What's all this about requirements and commitment?

—The employees are different from me. They are *(select any that apply)* younger, older, less educated, more educated, a different race or religion, from a different social or economic class, more or less knowledgeable about this community, etc.

—I am not sure what the employees really do. Am I doing their job? What are they doing while I do their job?

—Why should the salaried staff get paid while I don't (especially if I'm doing their job)?

—I am always told what to do, but am never asked to participate in planning the work.

—My suggestions are not listened to. People here seem unwilling to make changes.

—Employees get/take credit for my good ideas.

—No one says thank you.

—Volunteers always seem to get the "idiot work" around here.

—No one ever gives me feedback on my work. I wish I'd know how useful my efforts are or how I might improve my work.

—I am given jobs to do without being told their context, so I never really understand how my efforts fit into the activities of the organization.

—I always have to search for a place to do my work and there is nowhere to store my work from week to week.

—My grandmother founded this organization and these new staff members are not doing what she would have wanted.

—I should be treated as special because I am related to one of this group's *(select one:)* board members, donors, top executives, legislators.

—Salaried staff are always given the benefit of the doubt in any dispute. They are seen as "right" just because they are on the payroll.

—Whenever I come in, the employees are always at lunch, on a break, or in a meeting. Don't they ever do any work?

—I am given very little training or even good instructions. I am not sure who to ask if I have a question, especially if my supervisor is at lunch, on a break, or in a meeting.

—The staff is moody and often does not say hello, goodbye or thank you.

—I do not know who runs this place. A lot of people come and go from the front office, but I've never been told who they are. They rarely greet me in the hall.

—I don't like the label "volunteer." Can't I have a title?

—I'm just a volunteer.

Of course, you may be heading an organization in which there are many more volunteers than employees. In such circumstances, the salaried staff realize that volunteers are vital, but some volunteers may misinterpret their numerical strength and feel superior to the employees. This manifests itself in volunteers "giving orders" to the staff or resisting when staff delegates work to volunteers.

Diagnosis

The litany of possible attitudes just presented is intended to demonstrate how wide a range of causes there might be for tension between employees and volunteers. View both lists as a sort of "menu" from which to select the specific issues that might be at work in each tense situation. The dynamics of a particular confrontation will be unique to the individuals involved. And keep in mind that *veteran volunteers* can display the same reaction to "newcomer" volunteers as the salaried staff do! As CEO, much will depend upon your skill in diagnosing what is really going on beneath the surface.

Research what the actual circumstances are and therefore which attitudes stem from facts or myths. If a person has had a negative experience, it is unrealistic to expect him or her to be completely open to a second try. For example, if a salaried staff member worked hard to train a new volunteer and then that volunteer left the agency unexpectedly, it is obvious that the staff member will be wary of the commitment of future volunteers.

Sometimes it is helpful to consider why certain salaried staff members or volunteers are exceptionally receptive to teamwork with each other. Knowing the reasons for *good* relationships can indicate approaches to take to change negative relationships. Possible factors that would make for favorable support of volunteer involvement include:

—Personal history with volunteerism in another setting—if that past experience was positive.

—Respect for the work of the director of volunteers.

—Direct experience with excellent volunteers or salaried staff (as opposed to direct experience with mediocre volunteers).

—Praise from an executive for innovative work done with/by volunteers.

Middle Manager Attitudes

As you diagnose the causes of employee resistance, also assess the attitudes of people in middle management positions. These department heads and unit supervisors set the tone in their areas, conveying overt and subtle messages about work expectations. All too often, middle managers become the obstacle to effective volunteer involvement by not supporting paid staff's attention to volunteers. Unit supervisors may feel that volunteers drain staff time from priority work. Because these supervisors evaluate employee performance, they have substantial influence over how staff in their units approach all their responsibilities. Middle managers therefore are a vital—and often overlooked—link in how creative a unit is in designing assignments for volunteers, how well the unit trains and supervise volunteers, and whether paid staff feel appreciated for their efforts in welcoming volunteers.

Include middle managers in planning sessions, training, and evaluation so that they feel ownership of volunteer participation in their unit. Make sure they, too, receive personal recognition for their efforts. They need to see that volunteers help their department to "shine" and are contributing to, not diverting from, accomplishing goals.

In the next chapter we'll examine some of the other considerations that make for positive reinforcement of volunteer/salaried staff teamwork.

STRATEGIES TO CREATE TEAMWORK

As chief executive, you have a vital role to play in laying the groundwork for productive teamwork between salaried and volunteer staff. There are several concrete things you can do to establish policy and standards for your organization.

Job Descriptions: Employees

First, you can make certain that all job descriptions for employees include a statement about volunteers. In some cases, the job description will indicate that a staff member will have responsibility for supervising volunteers personally. In other cases, job descriptions may simply note that this is an organization in which volunteers are active and therefore all employees will have to interact positively with them. For department heads or middle managers, the job description might clarify that volunteers will be active in each component of the organization and that the department head will be expected to develop appropriate job descriptions, delegate work to volunteers, and help those they supervise to work effectively with volunteers.

If all employee job descriptions contain references to interaction with volunteers, then the job application process should also attempt to uncover a candidate's background in volunteerism. For example, include a question on the written application form that asks about the candidate's personal volunteer experience (you will undoubtedly discover many valuable things about the person's interests and other job-related qualifications from this question, as well as gain a sense of this person's understanding of the concept of volunteerism). In the interview, you should ask whether the candidate has ever supervised volunteers and in what context. It is helpful to ascertain whether the applicant has ever received formal training in volunteer management, either in a classroom setting (unlikely) or on the job in another organization.

Job Descriptions: Volunteers

In the volunteer management profession, there is universal agreement that volunteers deserve written job descriptions. Such descriptions clarify roles and differentiate what volunteers do from what employees do.[1] Writing down an assignment is not a paperwork exercise. It provides a tool that will be used in recruiting the right volunteer, in determining the necessary training for the job, in holding the staff accountable for supervising the volunteer, and for evaluating the work performed. Therefore it is also the basis for recognizing the achievements of a volunteer, or for initiating the process of termination.

The volunteer job description allows the director of volunteers to conduct a meaningful interview with an applicant. It demonstrates that your organization is not simply looking for people to "help out," but expects productive work to be accomplished. On this basis, it is possible to screen out prospective volunteers who do not fulfill the job description's qualifications— without creating any bad will for turning away someone who offers assistance. You set standards from the beginning.

The salaried staff member who will be working with the volunteer directly must be involved in writing the job description. This presupposes two requirements:

1) that the staff member's own work is efficiently organized so that someone else can assist with it; and

2) that the person is skilled in task analysis and can divide the work into manageable pieces to be delegated.

The latter is why the director of volunteers has an important role in helping the supervisor to define a reasonable, appropriate volunteer assignment. Having to write something down is a good way to insure that there is indeed a meaningful job to be done.

As CEO, you should stress the value of written volunteer job descriptions. See to it that time is taken to articulate these correctly and that they are reviewed as often as necessary to remain current. This action alone may alleviate many of the problems between volunteers and salaried staff. When people know what is expected of them, they are happier and more productive.

By the way, think about showing volunteers the job descriptions of the salaried staff, too. This makes the circle of understanding complete and documents that volunteers fulfill roles that are different from, but parallel to, those of the employees.

Be a Role Model

One wonderful way to demonstrate your commitment to volunteer involvement is to develop assignments with which volunteers can help *you*, at the executive level. Expect other management staff to do the same. This shows that volunteers are integrated throughout the organization, not colleagues from which frontline staff will eventually be "promoted out" of having to work alongside.

What are some things that the right volunteer might do for you? Consider:

—Design and possibly run surveys of many types: client satisfaction; public image; donor interests.

—Research local economic and demographic data to alert the agency to possible trends that will affect it.

—Read through the growing stack of professional journals and annotate articles of direct interest to your setting.

—Visit community agencies to bring back updated information on available resources.

—Write speeches.

If you feel some discomfort at the thought of sharing your own work, you will understand the reactions of the rest of staff.

Do a reality check and see if following good volunteer management practices leads to a successful relationship. Think about how nice it would be to move some projects off your "wish list" and on to someone's "to do" list.

Training   Once you have stated the expectation that salaried staff will work with volunteers, make certain that all present employees understand *how* to work with volunteers. Keep in mind that almost no one receives training in volunteer management as part of formal schooling and so there should be no shame in admitting uncertainty about successful techniques of volunteer supervision. If the staff are in any profession dealing in human services, be alert to resistance to the notion that their interpersonal skills need some sharpening! Social work begins at home, and many people who provide wonderful service to "clients" are unable to develop teamwork with those they label (often incorrectly) as "nonprofessionals."

The only way to be certain that staff will approach volunteer supervision consistently and in accordance with your policies is to provide training. The key is to demonstrate the importance of the subject by allocating time to it. Remember, very few staff will have learned the techniques of volunteer management in their formal education and so people may be surprised that you are devoting several hours to this subject.

Staff training must deal with attitudes as well as with skill development. For example, uncovering the stereotypes that employees have about volunteers is the first step toward new understanding. One interesting way to approach the whole subject is to give employees the chance to talk about the volunteering that *they* are doing outside of the job (or something they have done in the past as a volunteer). This sets up the concept of the Golden Rule—comparing how the employee likes to be treated when s/he is a volunteer with how s/he treats volunteers in the agency. It breaks down the barriers of "us" and "them."

Directly confronting some of the fears and threats about volunteers is also healthy. Encourage negatives to surface in a constructive way. Voicing concerns often diffuses resistance;

there is a level of relief in being allowed to urge caution. The training session can demonstrate that thoughtful suggestions will always be welcome. Discuss the individual "pay-offs" for developing teamwork with volunteers and review the agency's benefits from involving volunteers.

Sometimes there is the problem of vocabulary. It is common to refer to salaried staff as the "professionals." One dictionary definition of "professional" is indeed "one who earns a salary for one's work." This is the distinction between "professional" and "amateur" athletes, for example. But another definition of the word "professional" is someone who has special *training*. Staff must be helped to see that not all volunteers are untrained. There are many volunteers who bring educational credentials and relevant work experience equivalent to (though not necessarily the same as) those of the paid staff, even if offering their services voluntarily to the organization. It is insulting and tension-producing to differentiate paid and unpaid staff with the word "professional."

By the way, once you have trained your current staff in volunteer supervision skills, do not overlook the possible training needs of new employees you may bring on board later. Be sure to include some time in the volunteer office in the orientation schedule of new staff members, so that the director of volunteers can brief the newcomer about the way in which volunteers are integrated into your organization's services. Assess whether the new person requires more in-depth training, especially since you cannot assume s/he learned about working with volunteers at a previous job.

On an ongoing basis, be sure to put the subject of volunteers onto the agenda of staff meetings periodically, if not regularly. This is another way to send the message that teamwork is expected and that good news and problems concerning volunteers are going to be discussed by everyone. Whenever feasible, invite volunteers to join staff meetings at which work in which they are involved will be considered. This is practical, day-to-day recognition of their contributions.

Pilot Testing

As already mentioned in the chapter on planning, it is always a good idea to start small by pilot testing new assignment areas for volunteers. If employees feel overwhelmed by a sudden influx of a cadre of volunteers, how can an effective partnership develop? Allow time for the integration of volunteers to take place and for paid staff to gain confidence in working collaboratively with volunteers.

Supervision

Salaried staff in general do not have to learn all the techniques of how to develop and run a volunteer program. That is the responsibility of the director of volunteers. But to accomplish specific jobs, the staff should feel comfortable in supervising and collaborating with volunteers as co-workers. All the principles of good supervision of employees operate with volunteers, too. However, there are some special considerations to supervising volunteers. These include:

- The need to create a positive working "atmosphere." Because volunteers come and go during the course of a day or week, they encounter the work environment of a particular period. If the work site tone is harried and hassled, it will affect volunteers' approach to their work, too. If some volunteers are on duty at lunch time and therefore always see the staff on "break," they will sense a different atmosphere than those who are scheduled at a peak client visitation time. Enthusiasm and energy are infectious and really help volunteers to feel motivated. (Creating a good atmosphere for volunteers is one of those elements of volunteer management that rub off beautifully on the salaried staff. Everyone benefits from a positive tone in the working environment.)

- Many volunteer assignments involve work to be done outside of the agency's offices. This type of field work includes such independent responsibilities as home visits to clients, solicitation calls on potential donors, leadership of group activities (clubs, sports teams, trips). It is quite possible for a volunteer to serve the organization entirely separated from the work site of the supervisor or staff liaison. This physical separation requires special consideration for defining lines of communication and accountability.

• Volunteers need accessibility to a supervisor or someone designated to answer questions. If an employee has a question and discovers her/his supervisor has gone out to a meeting, the question can wait until the next day. But a volunteer may only be in once a week. In that circumstance, having no one who can move the work forward can amount to a waste of a work day. It is not sufficient to have another staff member hand the volunteer a pile of work to do (though this is light years ahead of having the volunteer arrive only to discover no one remembered s/he was coming in and no work was left at all!). Concern must be shown for supporting the volunteer's accomplishment of the task.

• The volunteer's commitment of time should be respected. If there is no work to be done in the person's assignment area on a particular day, then the volunteer should, in all courtesy, be contacted and told of the problem. S/he can be given the option of revising her/his schedule for the week or of coming in anyway to do some other task. But it should not be assumed that all volunteers will do "anything" just to help out.

 As alluded to above, nothing is more undercutting of the volunteer's commitment than to arrive at the job and discover that no work has been prepared—in fact, to realize that the salaried staff had forgotten the volunteer was even due in. Watching the employee rush around to "pull something together" for the volunteer to do is hardly conducive to the feeling of really being needed.

• There is something in the volunteer world that I have always called "instant accountability." This refers to the reality that, in the supervision of employees, there is a margin for error that does not exist with the supervision of volunteers. If a supervisor is moody, uncommunicative, nasty, or leaves no work to be done in his/her absence, the salaried worker will not like it, but will tolerate it—or perhaps will "wait out" the mood until a better day. But the volunteer who is treated discourteously or is left with nothing to do is quite likely never to return to the organization again. This is not to imply that volunteers are thin-skinned. But if one gives one's time to a facility and then is treated poorly, why should one return? It is a form of masochism or martyrdom to wish to repeat a bad experience under those circumstances.

It might be a measure of a supervisor's skill to realize that every time a volunteer *returns* to an agency it is a compliment to what occurred on the previous visit.

- Volunteers have freedom of choice beyond what employees are usually given. Employees must complete a wide variety of mandated tasks, even some that are tedious or somewhat unpleasant. A volunteer is free to say no to an assignment, without jeopardizing his/her right to remain a volunteer. This does not mean that a volunteer can randomly select which parts of a task to do and which to ignore. But it does mean that the person can, within reason, select a particular assignment on which to concentrate time and effort.

- There is a degree of "socializing" that is part of volunteering. This can get out of hand, at which point it becomes a reasonable complaint of the employees. But, within bounds, it is fair for a volunteer to want to have some personal interaction during his or her scheduled work time. So long as this does not interfere with productivity, it means that the supervisor might show an interest in the volunteer's activities since last seeing him or her.

- Ongoing recognition, especially in the form of saying thank you, is important to supervising volunteers. In some ways this amounts to an "exit line" in which a person is acknowledged for his/her efforts that day and is encouraged to return. But the thank you has to be sincere. Remember that volunteers do not always see the way their work fits into the larger picture. By next week, the project handled this week may seem forgotten—unless the supervisor notes how the volunteer's effort enabled the entire workload to be completed. (Again, it would be nice to say thank you more often to employees, too.)

Two important concepts to keep in mind when supervising volunteers are *courtesy* and *self-fulfilling prophecy*. So many interpersonal relationships can be handled smoothly with politeness and friendliness. This is important for any human interaction, but with volunteers the need to be courteous is even more vital. Similarly, when one expects the best, one often gets the best. If one has a low level of expectation about volunteers, volunteers will act accordingly—largely because they will end up being poorly recruited, trained and supervised.

Employees often want to know if they may criticize a volunteer. The answer is: of course. In fact, it is a form of compliment to give a person suggestions for improving work done; it implies that the supervisor has confidence that the volunteer has the capability and will to do a better job. And then the volunteer knows the work is important enough to be reviewed and done to the best of everyone's ability. Empty thank you's without enthusiasm leave volunteers with the uncomfortable suspicion that their work will be tossed out after they leave. It is better to deal directly with improving a volunteer's work. After all, when people give their time freely, it is in the hope that their effort will produce results—not to waste their time doing something wrong or ineffectively.

One useful tip is to require every new volunteer, regardless of status or background, to be a "trainee" for the first month or so of work. You might even distribute colorful "hi, I'm new here" buttons to cheerfully set the tone. All newcomers understand that they are in training, if only to become oriented to the organization. For the paid staff, the volunteer trainee period gives permission to correct early mistakes and give instructions.

Liaison Supervision by the Director of Volunteers

The director of volunteers maintains an ongoing relationship with volunteers placed throughout the organization and monitors the progress of volunteer assignments. The immediate staff supervisor is responsible for day-to-day supervision, specific to the job to be done. Should any problem arise, that supervisor is the first line of communication and accountability. However, the director of volunteers can be helpful to both the employee and the volunteer by being a third party to differences of opinion.

If the volunteer wishes to change assignments, it would be up to the director of volunteers to weigh the request and act upon it. Similarly, if the staff member wishes the volunteer transferred or terminated, the director of volunteers must be involved. Ideally, the interrelationship is cooperative and open, and not unlike the way in which a personnel or human resources department operates.

Collaboration with Volunteers

Not all volunteers work "under" salaried staff supervision. There are many assignments that utilize volunteers as independent specialists, consultants, or project leaders. These job descriptions genuinely imply partnership between volunteers and employees, on an equal footing. In fact, in some cases the volunteer's position (and expertise) may place him or her above the salaried staff member in rank. (See Chapter 8 for a discussion of board roles as one example.)

The principles of good volunteer "supervision" create effective teamwork, too. Clear job descriptions, respect for the volunteer's time and contributions, plus a willingness to be honest about the value of the work produced, encourage successful collaboration. One special need in these types of assignments is clarification of how the volunteer will keep the organization informed about her or his activities. Specify a *two-way* reporting process and timetable.

Once you have seen to it that all **Enforcement and**
staff receive the necessary training **Recognition**
in how to work with volunteers,
the next step is to enforce the
process by evaluating salaried staff on whether they are carrying
out this job function appropriately. Employees should receive
feedback on their effectiveness with volunteers as a part of any
annual or periodic performance review. This implies further that
exceptional effort and achievement with volunteer assistance will
receive special recognition (a raise, promotion, or at least a com-
ment)—and that poor teamwork will also carry negative sanctions. Only when good behavior is reinforced and bad behavior
carries consequences do an organization's standards carry weight.
Unless you are willing to act in this manner, you are only giving
lip service to "support" of volunteers—and the paid staff will each
decide unilaterally whether or not to cooperate with volunteers.
Without the risk of administrative disapproval, it is easy to opt for
not working with volunteers.

A workshop participant testified to the validity of this point
by telling the group that he was a retired Army officer who had
at one time been in charge of an installation in Europe. In this
position he acted as a sort of "mayor," responsible not only for
the soldiers but also for their civilian families and their activities,
including everything from Little League to the PTA. Each year the
Army offered a training course on "How to Work with Resident
Families" and each year it was cancelled for lack of attendance.
Then all commanders received a Pentagon memo noting that
from now on all commanders would be evaluated on how well
they supported civilian activities on post. That year, two sections
of the training course were sold out! It was not that civilians were
unimportant before the memo, it was simply that—given a multitude of responsibilities—he and his colleagues would give priority to those of clear importance to their superiors.

To be fair, enforcement is a two-way street. Volunteers
should also be held to high standards and there should be consequences if productivity is low or work is not done properly. If
some volunteers show poor attendance or resist instruction, they
should be informed of the organization's dissatisfaction. This is as
important as providing recognition for volunteers who do well. In
fact, it makes annual recognition events more meaningful if
everyone knows that mediocre volunteers were weeded out.
Employees will be more likely to accept evaluation of their abil-

ity to work successfully with volunteers if they know that the same assessment will be made of volunteers. Otherwise you are sending a mixed message: we want you to accept volunteers as equals, but we won't hold them to equal standards.

Pay-Offs to Individual Employees   Naturally you do not want employees to team with volunteers just because there is punishment for not doing so. Rather, you hope salaried staff see the benefits of volunteers to the organization and themselves. But it is important to remember that the benefits to the *agency* for involving volunteers are not at all the same as the "pay-offs" to an *individual* employee who takes the time to supervise volunteers well. For example, just because the agency might receive good public relations from informed community volunteers, it does not follow that a particular salaried staff member feels rewarded directly for the effort of working well with volunteers.

What are some of the benefits or "pay-offs" to an *individual employee?* Consider the following:

—When a staff member supervises volunteers well, s/he demonstrates to administration (you!) that s/he has managerial ability.

—Supervising volunteers is, indeed, on-the-job training for supervising employees.

—Volunteers bring a freshness of approach that can help the employee to see his/her work in a new way.

—Volunteers share the staff member's interests and can therefore reduce isolation and provide support in a way staff in other departments cannot.

—Since volunteers provide the luxury of trying new service approaches without the agency having to seek funding first, volunteers can test a new idea and prove its merit. If the idea to be demonstrated is the employee's, s/he has the chance to show her/his value to the organization.

—Volunteers can lessen the workload by handling a variety of helpful tasks.

—Volunteers can free the employee to do things s/he is specially trained for or likes.

—Both of the above can reduce employee tension and prevent burnout.

—Qualified volunteers can handle aspects of the work for which the employee may actually not be trained or best suited.

—Volunteers can stimulate creativity by adding new ideas and responding to staff innovations.

—Because volunteers may have a range of different life experiences, working together can provide personal enrichment for the staff.

Settling Disputes

Just because someone is a member of the salaried staff does not necessarily make his or her point of view "right" or more worthy of consideration if it differs from that of a volunteer. Intellectually this point might be acceptable but, in practice, management actions can imply that employees get the primary benefit of the doubt.

It is true that full-time employees, or even part-time employees with weekly schedules, see a broader picture than a volunteer with limited time on-site can. Also, demonstrating loyalty to a staff member with seniority is understandable. But every situation must be weighed in terms of its particular details, so as to insure that volunteers are not discriminated against.

How does such discrimination occur? One example is the case of a large metropolitan hospital in which the director of volunteers received a memorandum from an administrative assistant in another department concerning access to the photocopying machine. The memo asked the director of volunteers to instruct all volunteers whose assignments included photocopying to stop their work whenever a salaried staff member came to the copying room and to turn the machine over to the employee. In other words, the administrative assistant felt that employees had "first rights" to the copying machine. What are the underlying assumptions of this memo?

First, the memo implies that the time of the employees is "clearly" more valuable than that of the volunteers (after all, they have the time to volunteer, so they can wait around, right?). Second, the memo shows misunderstanding of what volunteers are doing in the photocopying room: they are (surprise!) making photocopies. And these copies are being made for departments/employees who need them as part of the hospital workload. So first come, first served is a reasonable rule in the photocopy room, no matter what the hourly rate of the person making the copies.

Actually, the full-time employee has more options as to when to return to the copying room. The volunteer, with a limited daily schedule, needs to complete as much work as possible in the allotted time. So asking the volunteer to wait around while the employee does copying turns out to be more wasteful of productivity than may be realized.

The most notable fact about this memo is that it was sent at all, in the complacent certainty that the salaried staff had the right to dictate the use of organizational resources. It expressed the opinion that volunteers should do "whatever it is they do" only when it does not "interfere" with the really important activities of the employees. The way to begin to deal with such attitudes is to recognize them when they surface. As chief executive, you have the chance on a daily basis to reaffirm that volunteers are legitimate workers with equal access to resources. If the volunteers' assignments are appropriately planned, their need for workspace, supervision, and even copying machines can be accommodated with a minimum of stress.

If individual disputes occur between a member of the salaried staff and a volunteer, these should be handled in the same manner as any interpersonal problem. The two people should first be encouraged to work out their differences together. It should not be acceptable for the employee to unilaterally decide: "I just can't work with this volunteer; ask him/her to leave." If necessary, the employee's immediate supervisor can mediate the problem, possibly also calling in the director of volunteers for assistance. The volunteer's point of view deserves to be heard and to be evaluated on its own merit. Of course, if there are facts that the volunteer is unaware of because of his/her limited schedule or other considerations, these should be explained. But again the bottom line is that a salaried staff member cannot rely on being seen as "right" *a priori* on the basis of being on the payroll.

If volunteers are indeed in the wrong, the staff should feel that standards will be maintained and that such nonproductive or counter-productive workers will be asked to leave. It is probably necessary to mention that volunteers should also not be protected against criticism or even "firing" simply out of gratitude for their voluntary service. Reassignment of a volunteer to a new unit or to a new staff supervisor may be an appropriate way of solving a particular interpersonal problem. But reassignment should not be expected "on demand" of an employee. This is another version of giving staff all the power with no accountability for their skills in supervision.

Unions

If labor unions are active in your facility, the question of volunteers will come up sooner or later in contract negotiations. There are just as many examples of peaceable relations between union employees and volunteers as there are examples of tension. The way to insure peace is to *plan in advance.*

Bring up the subject of volunteers well before labor relations become problematic. There are really only two issues about volunteers that concern union leaders: will volunteers be used to replace employee positions, reduce overtime pay, or prevent new salaried positions from being created; and what will be the role of volunteers during a possible employee strike?

The latter is simpler to handle than the former. The basic rule about utilization of volunteers in a strike is to treat volunteers as individuals capable of making their own decisions. If volunteers wish to continue with their ongoing assignments during a strike, they should be permitted to do so as a matter of personal choice. However, administration might assure union members that no new volunteers will be recruited or mobilized during a strike—nor will volunteers already on board be re-assigned to cover work that strikers normally handle. The bottom line for unions is to receive assurance that volunteers will not be utilized as *strike breakers* to provide the agency with a work force capable of holding off the strikers for a long period of time.

It is legitimate to agree to thoughtful utilization of volunteers during a strike as much for protection of the volunteers as out of fairness to employees. But on the other hand, do not agree to refuse to allow volunteers admittance to the facility if a strike is on—this violates each volunteer's right to choose his or her own position.

The question of "taking jobs" is much more difficult to clarify because almost every organization utilizes volunteers as a way to stretch the budget beyond what available money would otherwise be able to "buy" through employees. While each administrator must honestly deal with the suspicion that volunteers will be used as a way to *cut* a budget, at the same time it is justifiable to firmly assert the position that management has the right to locate and utilize whatever resources will allow the organization to meet its goals and serve its clientele.

Here is an area in which volunteer job descriptions are invaluable. Administration should be able to document that it is the intent of the organization to recruit and assign volunteers to positions that are substantially *different from* the roles filled by employees. This does not mean that all volunteer positions have to be "subservient" to employees. It simply means that the slots to be filled by salaried staff are the ones shown in the budget and that the job descriptions written for volunteers would not be filled by employees under most circumstances. Employees and volunteers may share specific tasks, but have discrete and different roles.

It is probably useful to clarify with union representatives whether or not volunteers will be utilized as a temporary measure if an employee leaves a job, until a paid replacement is found.

To prevent future tension, it might be helpful to encourage union representation on any advisory committee or evaluation team supporting the volunteer office. But beware of giving the union the power to OK or veto volunteer job descriptions. If your policy of not duplicating staff roles is accepted, the day-to-day implementation of this should not be given to the union for oversight.

Perhaps this is a good point to discuss legitimate concerns about
budget cutting, since employees
are so often wary of new volunteer

Budget Cutting

projects because of questions of job security. Many organizations
are faced with an impossible choice: the need to reduce spending while maintaining or even increasing services. Some groups
may wish to expand services but recognize that additional funding will be hard to find. This is the type of situation in which it
is very appealing to conclude that "we'll do it all with volunteers."
The fallacy of this simplistic approach has already been discussed. Volunteers may be "free" in the sense of not requiring a
great deal of cash outlay, but they are very expensive in terms of
recruitment, training, coordination, and supervision time.

As an overall observation, don't wait until a budget crisis to
begin to involve volunteers. This reinforces the notion that volunteers are a second-choice Band-Aid. Not only will staff resist
volunteer help just when they themselves are coping with an
increased workload, but it is hard to sound sincere when recruiting in desperation. The best way to gain expanded volunteer
support in lean times is to have incorporated volunteers as a welcome resource much earlier.

If you are faced with staff layoffs, can you turn to volunteers for help? It is next to impossible to "fill a gap" left by a full-
time employee with only one qualified and available volunteer—
it would require an intricate schedule of several volunteers each
giving a certain number of hours per week and each bringing the
organization a different set of qualifications. Take all the concerns
of "job sharing" and multiply them several fold!

It is also a mistake to assume that somehow it will be easier to find volunteers to handle the low-level, clerical jobs of the
agency. Under this assumption, when the budget diminishes, all
the "professional" staff are retained but the secretaries are let go.
The irony is that the organization can survive more reasonably if
the public relations staff is cut back or if there are three fewer
caseworkers than by losing someone to answer the telephone
during all working hours! Equally ironically, it is easier these days
to find volunteers willing to handle the more challenging assignments of, say, writing the organization's newsletter or helping a
family to learn budgeting than to get a full shift of volunteers to
do data entry or envelope stuffing.

The best way to handle the real problem of a reduced budget is to reassess the job descriptions of the *entire staff.* This means doing a task analysis of the way things really work in the organization, not just what was put on paper in the distant past. Scrutinize the various tasks that each employee is doing and identify the following sorts of things:

—What is someone doing once a week or periodically, rather than daily or on an inflexible schedule?

—What is someone doing that really does not require his or her specialized training? (For example, a lot of time is spent in making follow-up telephone calls, composing letters, etc. that may take someone away from direct service to clients.)

—What is someone doing that might be done more effectively by someone else with special training in that skill?

Once you have identified these specific tasks, you are ready to re-align all the job descriptions. *Re-write employee positions* so that these contain all the tasks that require daily attention, special training, etc. Add the similar critical responsibilities that had been assigned to the "cut" staff members, so that the remaining employees are primarily now assigned to the most vital, daily functions. Remove the other periodic or less technical responsibilities—which then become the basis for legitimate *volunteer* job descriptions. You will be asking volunteers to handle work (still important) that can be done on a once-a-week basis or that makes use of special talents for which the volunteers have been recruited.

This approach to the unfortunate need to trim the budget is therefore good management of both salaried and volunteer staff. You will be paying for the best utilization of your employees and will attract volunteers in support of your organization. It is also hard for unions to be as negative about this approach, though careful negotiation is probably in order.

One last observation about retrenchment. Unfortunately, it is not unusual to see organizations lay off their director of volunteers in the first round of staff cuts. The theory is that the director of volunteers is "indirect" staff and that, since there are already volunteers in place, there will be few immediate consequences because of this vacancy. Then, often without seeing the irony, these same organizations also announce that they are seeking more volunteers! Clearly it is my position that the more critical volunteers are to your organization, the more important the position of the person who leads the volunteer program. Not only do you need such a manager to expand the volunteer corps, but current volunteers can feel unsupported and taken for granted when they lose their staff liaison. On the other hand, if you are laying off employees in large numbers, this is probably not the most diplomatic time to *create* a new position of director of volunteers! So again, plan for volunteers when times are good if you want their help in times of crisis.

Teamwork Prognosis

When analyzed in the way we have just been doing, the factors that affect teamwork between volunteers and salaried staff are not mysterious. In many ways they are the same factors involved in the interrelationships of members of the salaried staff. The major difference is that people expect to define paid work roles, but too often overlook the same need for clarification of volunteer roles. Assumptions fill the gap when there are no established policies— assumptions that may well be wrong.

While some initial tension between volunteers and employees may be understandable, there are equally important benefits to each for establishing a sense of partnership. By paying attention to the issues just described, the outlook is very positive for real integration of paid and volunteer staff.

Finally, it is worth re-emphasizing that the last two chapters have contained concepts basic to good management— regardless of whether or not the workers to be managed are volunteers or employees. The most effective ways to support volunteers are also the best ways to work with paid staff—not the other way around. The organization that creates a positive working atmosphere for its volunteers usually also benefits from the high morale and productivity of its employees.

---

[1]For more discussion about how to delineate roles for volunteers and employees, see *Building Staff/Volunteer Relationships* by Ivan H. Scheier, Energize, 1993.

SPECIAL CATEGORIES OF VOLUNTEERS

One of the most exciting things about involving volunteers is that the potential for tapping the resources of your community is limitless. When you develop a volunteer program, you give its leader the mandate to recruit whatever assistance can effectively meet your organization's needs. This opens the door to all sorts of creative utilization of people and cooperation with other organizations. Avoid defining "volunteers" too narrowly. Seek out the widest range of community resources through your volunteer program office.

We have already recognized that volunteers come with every possible type of background and characteristics. In this chapter, we'll examine some special categories of volunteers that are legitimately recruited and administered through your director of volunteers, but which require some top executive involvement in decision making and policy setting.

Students

As CEO, you define the categories of workers in your organization. If your agency is a placement site for college or graduate students completing "internships," there may be some debate over whether or not these students should be coordinated by the volunteer program office. Coordination of student interns is an administrative issue that is separate from the question of who should supervise such students once they are working in the organization. Do not allow the waters to be muddied by either the academic institution or various "professionals" in your agency. The volunteer office has a clear and supportive role to play in the effectiveness of internships...and here is why:

- From the point of view of payroll, student interns are just as much "volunteers" as any other volunteer. Interns work in the agency for benefits other than financial reward. Academic credit cannot be negotiated at the store for a loaf of bread.

- There are indeed differences between student interns and other volunteers, but these are considerations related mainly to what the interns will be asked to do and who will supervise them. Often a school will ask for special training experiences to make the internships more valuable. In terms of management, these considerations are not very different from the need to match any volunteer to the best assignment or to accommodate such factors as physical disability. The volunteer office, therefore, can keep the list of all available internship job descriptions and do *initial screening* of all applicants. Then it should be up to the actual staff supervisor to make the final decision on *acceptance* of the intern (just as with any volunteer who would be assigned to a unit).

- By utilizing the volunteer office to centralize all internship applications, you save staff time in contact with the various colleges and you make sure that any internship applicant is told of *all* available openings. If individual staff supervisors make the first contact, they will only be aware of what is available in their one particular unit and will not offer the prospective intern the full range of assignment options for the entire organization. Similarly, if a student is not right for one unit, only the volunteer office has the overview necessary to see if there is another possible placement that would be more appropriate.

- If you do not utilize the volunteer office, where will records be kept on student interns? Is anyone keeping such records at all now? As executive, don't you want to know how much staff time is being spent on interns, how many students you have assisted, or what the performance level of interns has been? If for no other reason, it may be necessary to document the work of interns to meet insurance requirements (since, as with all volunteers, there are accident and liability considerations for interns).

- Many student interns contribute far more hours to the agency than the minimum required by the school. Is this extra time not "volunteering" in its purest sense? Also, a percentage of students will want to remain active with the agency after the official end of their internships. Will you then expect them to "transfer" to the volunteer office—or will they remain undocumented (and, actually, unauthorized) in an unclassified state? In one workshop I taught, a participant admitted that she knew of at least three students who had kept right on with their work for over a year after their school ties had ended, but no one reported it until she asked why the young people were still around. Some of their co-workers in the unit were not even aware that the official internship had ended. Parenthetically, is this the best way to help students with their education? Maybe these students were ready to move on to more challenging assignments in another part of the organization, but no one was "responsible" for making this offer to them.

- Every newcomer to the agency deserves an orientation. If interns by-pass the volunteer office and go directly to their line supervisors, they will not get an overview of the entire organization. The volunteer program is already set up to offer orientation and students should have access to it. Training for the specific task to be done will be given by the supervisor, as is appropriate.

- From a public relations standpoint, if you do not centralize the coordination of internships in the volunteer office, you are expecting the various schools and colleges to track down as many staff supervisors as necessary to place what may be several students. Working through the volunteer office would allow the faculty to make one contact a semester, referring all the student internship candidates at one time. Similarly, requests for end-of-placement evaluations can be channelled through the volunteer office (one call for the school), so that the director of volunteers can monitor whether all forms have been submitted as required. Copies of such evaluations can then be kept in the volunteer office with the student intern's other records, so that future references can be made easily.

- A number of years ago, the only student internships were those in medicine, nursing, teaching and social work, and the type of placement and professional expertise of the required supervisor were clearly defined. Today, there are "internships" in a wide variety of subjects ranging from geography to communications. These newer internships are not always so definitive in requiring that a supervisor offer a fixed professional background. Whether the internship is of the "traditional" kind or the more unstructured, experiential learning kind, the volunteer office is your agency's best vehicle for screening applicants and determining suitable assignments.

- Finally, without the involvement of the volunteer office, it is unlikely that students will receive formal recognition of their accomplishments during their internships. Only you and the volunteer office can represent the entire agency in expressing appreciation.

Apart from internships in which the student is committed to a specific schedule for a duration of time, there is also the question of student "observers." You should have some policy defining your organization's point of view on such observation, largely because it is time-consuming for the staff without necessarily contributing anything to service. Once again, the most logical administrative umbrella for student observers is the volunteer office. The director of volunteers can make the arrangements with the school, schedule appropriate visits, keep records of the activity, and perhaps even recruit some of the students as ongoing volunteers!

Many high schools and even some junior high, middle, and

elementary schools have instituted a variety of what are often called "community service" programs. These range from curriculum-based, "service-learning" activities to completely optional volunteer work coordinated through the school. A recent but growing trend is to mandate a set number of service hours as a requirement for graduation. Here is where the debate over who is a "volunteer" may surface, since many educators want to distinguish the community service of students from what they perceive as low-level help by traditional "volunteers." No matter what you call the contributions of students, it is still important to connect them to your volunteer program office for all of the reasons just discussed.

Stipended Workers

At various times your agency may have access to volunteers who receive a stipend for their work. The stipend is never more and often less than minimum wage and is intended to enable the person to give a considerable number of hours of service in lieu of another, more lucrative job or as a supplement to a low income. Sometimes a living allowance for expenses is included. Most often such money comes from government programs and usually the agency contributes some percentage of matching funds.

Stipended workers are considered part of the volunteer world because the amount of money they receive is always considerably less than the professional nature of their job would ordinarily command and because they choose to participate in such service for a set period of time (usually one to two years). The Peace Corps and VISTA pioneered such efforts; the more recent AmeriCorps continues the tradition. Whatever Congressional budgeting decides, it is likely that some form of full-time, stipended "national service" program will continue or be reinvented in the future. Other established projects such as Foster Grandparents are also likely to continue.

From the perspective of this book, the important thing is to consider, first, whether your agency wants to seek such special categories of workers. They do provide a considerable number of hours each week, with some continuity, as well as offer a generally enthusiastic participant. Second, recognize the stipended worker's similarity to volunteers—much as we just examined student interns. Only the volunteer office has the system in place to orient and place people who do not fit into the conventional employment structure.

Corporate **Volunteerism**
Community-conscious businesses have long participated in charitable efforts. Starting in the Reagan administration, however, corporate philanthropic efforts received increased attention. The phrase "corporate volunteerism" refers to the involvement of a company's employees as volunteers in community organizations. Of course employed people have always been active as volunteers, but "corporate volunteerism" implies that the company itself, as the employer, takes a direct role in encouraging the public service involvement of its workers. It has also come to be an umbrella term for some of the in-kind services businesses provide at no cost to nonprofit organizations.

From the purview of this book, what is important about corporate volunteerism is that you and your director of volunteers may have to work cooperatively in approaching corporations for assistance. You may be requesting a financial contribution from a company, but may also want to recruit its employees (or retirees) as volunteers. It is important to present a unified management team, rather than find your organization has contacted a corporation from several angles at once—looking as though the left hand does not know what the right hand is doing. Also, it is becoming more and more usual for a business to respond to a request for money by offering a "package" of funds, in-kind services, and employee volunteers. As executive, will you be able to utilize such a package effectively without planning together with the director of volunteers?

There is no reason to make corporate volunteers into a special category all by themselves, even if the employees are given "release time" or "flex time" by the corporation. If they are going to fill existing volunteer job descriptions, they should be integrated into your organization's corps of volunteer workers, just as would volunteers from any source. In most cases the company employees will actually be volunteering on their own time, so there is even less reason to differentiate them from other volunteers. The only exception might be technical assistance volunteers, which we will discuss in a moment.

When the director of volunteers seeks volunteer assistance for your organization, s/he often uncovers ways to get needed services at no cost or at highly reduced cost. Such development of in-kind contributions is a part of the role of the director of volunteers which you should cultivate and support. It is one of the sometimes hidden aspects of the job that can be misinterpreted as overstepping boundaries (since the director of volunteers is generally not authorized to "fund raise"). Here is another context in which the department of volunteers is really the "department of donated community resources." A creative director of volunteers will turn up in-kind, barter, exchanges, collaborations, loans, *and* volunteers.

Technical Assistance Volunteers

In a number of communities, special projects are functioning that recruit highly-skilled volunteers willing to provide technical assistance consultation on a short-term basis to any agency with need for such help. This also gives the volunteers the chance to donate their expertise to a wide variety of community agencies. Such programs may be run by a Volunteer Center as a "skills bank" or by a local chapter of AARP or Executive Service Corps. Some corporations have established their own skills banks, registering interested employees and then informing local agencies of the types of skills obtainable. Another source of management-level volunteers may be your area's Community Leadership program, often sponsored through the Chamber of Commerce.

Some of the skills offered are concrete, such as carpentry, art talent, or computer programming. For such talents, it is not difficult to create suitable volunteer assignments and evaluate success. The bookshelves are built, the brochure designed, the records entered. However, many of the skills available are less tangible and more managerial, ranging from expertise in strategic planning to personnel policy development. This type of technical assistance implies that an organization is willing to open up its management process to consultation from the volunteer—and it means that the top administrators will be directly involved.

Working with a volunteer consultant is no different from working with a paid consultant in terms of the potential benefits from the shared expertise. Many of the techniques for maximizing paid consulting time also apply to getting the most from a volunteer expert: proper identification of the needs to be addressed; homework on your part to offer the consultant useful background materials; good agenda planning; follow-up of recommendations. But technical assistance from a volunteer does require some special attention to show that you value the volunteer's time and opinions as though you were indeed paying for these in cash.

Regardless of whether the technical assistance is provided to the vice president or the custodian, the director of volunteers has the same responsibilities in the process as with any other volunteer. The short-term technical assistance role is simply one more type of volunteer assignment. Even the management volunteer who will work directly with you, at the top, should not bypass the volunteer office.

Group Volunteering Many types of volunteer assignments bring together groups of volunteers to accomplish the work. Sometimes the volunteers are individuals who happen to be scheduled for the same shift, but sometimes an already-established community group agrees to provide several of its members to volunteer in your facility together. Whether the source is a church, synagogue, school, corporation, or civic organization, keep in mind that one of the reasons the source is supporting your volunteer project is to develop a sense of identity and unity among its own group members. This may or may not interfere with your desire to generate loyalty to your organization in people who contribute to you as volunteers.

All group volunteering is coordinated through the volunteer program office, but the point to remember as CEO is that your organization has formed a collaboration with another organization. Be sure that lines of authority and communication are defined, and that group volunteers receive the same orientation and training as would any other volunteer. Clarify possible issues such as insurance coverage, especially if organized groups participate in one-time special events, such as large fundraisers.

One special consideration in group volunteering is whether or not children are welcome to participate. Family volunteering can be wonderful and groups such as churches or even corporations encourage parents to include their sons and daughters in service projects. If youngsters are on site, do any special arrangements have to be made for safety, supervision, or even refreshments?

In the last few years a number of projects have emerged in cities around the country that capitalize on the reluctance of some people to commit to long-term volunteer assignments. Appealing especially to younger and busier businesspeople, such projects organize one-time group volunteer activities, often in the evening or on weekends. More than twenty communities now have a City Cares affiliate (like Philadelphia Cares or Hands On Atlanta) and hundreds of United Ways are sponsoring a "Day of Caring" each fall. While such one-shot events will not solve your staffing problems, be sure to investigate whether your agency can become a placement site. Apart from receiving an intensive burst of help (usually with physical work like vacant lot clean up), you get visibility as a worthwhile organization and volunteers can test the water to see if they might want to contribute more regularly to your agency.

Informal Volunteers

In the course of a program year, you may find that your organization benefits from the "help" of individuals who informally give a few hours of their time in some way (as you will have discovered if you conduct the inventory of present volunteers that I recommended in Chapter 2). Most often such volunteers are family members or friends of the staff or of current volunteers. And they frequently surface during major fundraising or public events, when your organization needs lots of support work such as carrying boxes, staffing booths, and cleaning up. Such informal contributions are wonderful. The only caveat is to assess the situation and make sure that, if someone is really serving for many hours on an annual basis, you are not simply permitting loose management just because the person is not on the payroll. If someone can be identified as volunteering, perhaps the volunteer program office should enroll him or her more formally. This permits better utilization of the volunteer, inclusion in the thank you's that follow an event, coverage by your insurance, and the most accurate documentation of community contributions to your organization.

Up to now I have maintained the party line about defining volunteer work carefully, writing volunteer job descriptions, and maintaining some sort of structure. For most types of organizations, this is the best way to involve volunteers effectively—and not waste their time.

But there are other ways to be successful, too. Some settings or certain areas of work lend themselves to a much more relaxed, drop-in sort of approach that may attract a wider range of volunteers than anything else. For example, if you are doing a lot of outdoor work requiring many hands, why not send out the word that *anyone and everyone* who shows up on Saturday afternoons is welcome? Work team captains should be recruited with job descriptions, training, and some longer-term commitment, but each week their labor pool will expand and contract, and change. It is true that some weeks will see fewer volunteers than needed and other weeks more. But the goals of generating neighborhood enthusiasm, accomplishing a bit each week, and being welcoming to everyone can be met.

Not every organization will have work conducive to this "throw out the rules" approach. But you may be surprised at what someone might be able to do to help if you are willing to loosen up. For example, can a volunteer bring a friend along one day even if that person has not applied or interviewed? For some jobs the best risk management answer has to be no. But for a lot of other work, the answer might be yes. Just be sure you *make the decision to be informal,* rather than lapse into it because no one is paying attention.

Court-Referred Volunteers

It has become customary for court systems to practice "alternative sentencing," in which an offender is given the option of completing a set number of hours of community service work in lieu of a fine or spending time in prison, or as an adjunct to probation or parole. The offenses committed range from misdemeanors to more serious crimes. There are many models of alternative sentencing programs, but all are looking for organizations willing to offer placements to program participants. (Note that the justice system has long referred to this as "community service," a fact that confuses and confounds educators now trying to establish that phrase to describe student projects.) The best programs give participants the chance to choose their assignments—and your organization always has the right to refuse individual applicants.

If you agree to accept court-referred volunteers, you will probably need to set related policy. Some of the policy areas to determine are:

—Whether you wish to place any limits on the nature of the offense or on the minimum amount of hours in the sentence. (For example, it may not be cost-effective for you to orient and place someone who has less than twenty hours of community service work to do, unless you have a number of short-term projects waiting to be tackled.)

—How much you need to know of the person's court record before placing him or her. Who in your organization will be told of the person's sentence and for what reasons.

—How you will handle possible infringements of the placement agreement, should they occur. For example, after how many absences will the probation officer or other court contact be notified?

—Whether court-referred workers will be assigned to the same jobs as other volunteers and how this might affect the overall volunteer program.

Once again, use the volunteer office as the conduit for these court-referred workers. They are nonsalaried, temporary personnel who require screening, orienting, etc., just as all other volunteers do. This is also a way to be sure the proper legal records are kept to verify the time served.

Interestingly, data on existing alternative sentencing programs indicate that a significant percentage of people referred by courts to do community service continue to be active as volunteers well after their mandatory time is over. This is a positive side-effect for both the person and the organization.

Residents or Clients   Another source of volunteers that
as Volunteers   you may need to clarify and define
                              is your client group itself. As a
                              special form of "self-help," you
may want to encourage the people who receive services to, in
turn, become givers by participating as volunteers. Some examples of this type of volunteering include:

—Retirement center residents taking an active role in visiting, feeding and helping other residents who are ill
  enough to be in the nursing care unit.

—Patients in a long-term mental health facility helping to
  tend the gardens and grounds.

—Students doing a major clean-up project within their
  school building.

—Residents in a home for those with severe disabilities
  forming a program committee to plan year-round special
  events.

—Seniors in a nutrition center helping to set the tables
  before and clean up after their lunch.

The common denominator of all these examples is that
there is a very fine line between what might be reasonably
"expected" from program participants versus what is some type
of "extra" service that warrants the label of "volunteer." Every
organization must come to its own definition of what makes a
resident or client a volunteer—and whether and how this group
of volunteers differs from "outside" volunteers. In practice, this
includes such questions as: will the residents who volunteered be
invited to the annual volunteer recognition event?
     Some of the types of resident or patient volunteering are
really an attempt to foster *participation* in the facility's program
so that the experience is more home-like or therapeutic. Other
types of client involvement encourage "ownership" of the activity and reduce the feeling that the person is receiving "charity."
Self-respect is thereby maintained while getting necessary work
done.

The key variable in all this is *choice*. Each person must participate completely voluntarily and should have as wide an array of options for particular assignments as possible. It is choice that places such activity within the realm of volunteering. At the same time, the agency also retains the right to assign (or reassign) a participant-volunteer or even to withdraw permission to be a volunteer if the person is not able to contribute effectively to service delivery to others. However, it is imperative that someone who is not eligible to volunteer in no way jeopardizes his or her right to remain a recipient of agency services.

Some organizations have run into difficulty implementing a client-as-volunteer program because of protests from those outside the facility. The major point raised by such protesters is that clients are being utilized as unpaid labor. Several court cases have successfully enjoined agencies from continuing certain types of programs using patients or residents as workers, unless a minimum wage is offered. In most of these cases, the evidence revolved around whether the clients truly had the choice to say no to the work activity.

If you wish to implement a self-help volunteer project, be sure to clarify the issues involved and to utilize the director of volunteers in establishing some structure. It would be highly appropriate to ask the clients themselves for input from the very beginning.

Vested-Interest Volunteers

Another group of potential volunteers with similarities to resident/client volunteers is people with a special or vested interest in your work. This includes family members of residents, patients, students, or other constituents of your facility. Such volunteers are motivated by the desire to support your work but also by concern for the welfare of their parent, child or other relative. The key is to assure that the latter does not overshadow the former.

Apply volunteer management principles. Clarify roles, channels for voicing complaints (or praise), and other working relationships. When is the relative acting as a volunteer and when as a consumer? Are all relatives welcome as volunteers or must they apply and be accepted into the program? Will the relative be assigned to work with his or her relation, or do you prefer that volunteers have some separation from their personal connections? What if the client or student prefers that his or her relative be assigned elsewhere?

Some of these policy decisions should be considered even if relatives volunteer only on a limited basis, such as parents chaperoning a class trip.

Volunteers may have an even more personal interest in your cause, although they may not currently be "clients." For example, health foundations have many volunteers who are themselves diagnosed with the disease being combatted. Domestic violence programs involve volunteers with histories of abuse who may still be in litigation against their spouses. Performing arts centers may attract the donated services of performers themselves as volunteers. Again, the more defined the roles of volunteers, the less chance for conflict of interest and the greater the chance for wonderful contributions. "Defining" roles does not mean "limiting" them!

Finally, what are the considerations when major donors wish to be active direct-service volunteers? The donor may be used to personal contact with you or the development office, but the chain of command is probably quite different in the volunteer assignment. Orient the donor about the demands of volunteer work and help paid staff to feel comfortable in supervising the work done by this volunteer.

Funded Jobs Programs

There are a number of federal, state and local government programs that pay participants a stipend or even a full salary to work in selected community agencies, most often as a form of job training. Such programs often are focused on a particular target population that is difficult to employ, such as teenagers, senior citizens, the disabled, or non-English speakers. As with the stipended forms of "national service" already mentioned, program models range from ones in which the recipient agency pays a percentage of the worker's salary to ones with no host financial obligation at all.

As CEO, you will need to make a determination as to which workers are to be considered employees and which volunteers. One reasonable approach would be to place any worker receiving financial payment under your personnel office, while placing non-remunerated workers under the volunteer office.

For bookkeeping purposes, this division on the basis of money works quite well, but there are other considerations to insure smooth organizational functioning. If the special salaried workers are part-time and/or not clearly skilled, perhaps the director of volunteers needs to be part of the assignment-making process regardless of who maintains chief responsibility for these workers. Once again, who else maintains an ongoing list of the available short-term work in the agency or is prepared to conduct an orientation at any time?

In addition, it is important to make sure that a temporary influx of stipended workers does not displace loyal volunteers. This does not mean that a new source of help should be turned down. It simply suggests that present volunteers should be considered in your planning process and should be approached for suggestions as to what they would most prefer doing, should they be "replaced" by paid newcomers.

Unemployment and Disability Service Plans

Since the first edition of this book, a number of states have integrated community service into their unemployment and public assistance programs. Under such plans, recipients of public monies are expected to demonstrate that they are taking steps to become independent. Their options include attending school or a training program, taking a part-time job, or performing a certain number of hours of "community service" as a volunteer. Ironically, other states legislate against volunteering by those receiving public funds because of the assumption that the time spent at the volunteer assignment takes away from the person's focus on finding a job.

If your state has a program under which people may do community service work—or are mandated to do it—does this provide a pool of possible workers for your organization? Just as with the other government programs already discussed, especially court-ordered service, your agency may have to verify and report on the work done by someone in such a program.

Similarly, some states allow and even encourage people on extended or permanent disability leave to do volunteer work.

Perhaps even more interesting, a small number of corporations have been pioneering the concept that, since they pay the bill for temporary disability leave, employees who are reasonably fit but not yet able to return to their regular jobs can be offered the chance or even required to volunteer in nonprofit agencies. The company sees this as a donation to the community, since they are funding the employee's time anyway.

Virtual Volunteering   The newest category of volunteering was not even imaginable as recently as three years ago because it has evolved as a direct result of computer technology and online interaction in cyberspace. In fact, a whole new term has been coined to identify "virtual volunteering." The volunteers are indeed real, but they contribute their services via computer linkup. So far, this is a truly innovative and experimental area, and all indications are that it will increase in the future.

Current examples of virtual volunteering include technical assistance provided by e-mail. People with professional expertise offer access to themselves for short answers to specific questions by organizations. Lawyers, accountants, marketing experts, real estate agents, and others register as being willing to accept questions. Obviously, the expert and the agency do not have to be anywhere near each other—in cyberspace, distance does not matter. So organizations can now tap into the technical assistance and creativity of an endless number of volunteers, providing that the help needed can be given online. As even more advanced technology becomes available, especially real-time video interface, the types of help that can be offered will also expand.

Another area of virtual volunteering is people-to-people contact. Whether a cyberspace version of a self-help group or one person "visiting" another, such contact will become more and more welcome as people grow comfortable with computer interaction.

Still one more use of online interaction is in fundraising. Not only do the Internet and the World Wide Web offer amazing outreach potential to uncover people who might support your work, but it is already possible to sponsor a "fundraiser" in cyberspace. For example, a California-based organization called

Impact Online sponsored "Cooking on the Net." In exchange for a financial contribution (through e-mail) in support of several charitable groups, donors received (also by e-mail) recipes donated by world-famous chefs (in this context, volunteers, of course).

Is your agency online? Did you ever consider the volunteer-related implications of this technology? Can your leader of volunteers innovate yet another way to do virtual volunteering? Note, too, that for a large number of agencies, it is knowledgeable volunteers who are giving their time and expertise to create Web pages and teach staff all about cyberspace.

Vision

If the director of volunteers is seen consistently as heading the organization's "Nonsalaried Personnel Department" or "Community Resources Department," the interrelationship of the above categories with more traditional sources of volunteers becomes apparent. Once you have made the various executive decisions necessary to authorize the director of volunteers to coordinate the full range of volunteers as just described, your organization will benefit from all available community resources on an ongoing basis.

Remember the mandate that I expressed at the beginning of this chapter. Expect your director of volunteers to do three things: proactively identify agency and client needs; design ways people can address those needs; and then mobilize non-cash community resources to meet those needs. Whether or not you (or they) use the word "volunteer" does not matter at all. The challenge is to expand your organization's vision about sources of help.

EXECUTIVE-LEVEL
VOLUNTEERS

This book is focused primarily on direct service or "in-house" volunteers. But most organizations also benefit from the services of another set of volunteers: those who make or affect policy, or who independently raise funds. All nonprofit organizations have a board of directors whose members are volunteers. Many organizations also have an auxiliary or other fundraising body, usually organized as a self-led group of volunteers. Finally, a wide variety of advisory councils involve community members. For some units of government, such advisory councils may even be mandated by law as an opportunity for citizen participation.

In almost all cases, the top executive is the connecting link between such volunteers and the rest of the organization. In this chapter, we'll examine how the principles relating to in-house volunteers apply equally to these special types of volunteers.

THE BOARD

There is a growing body of literature about the work of nonprofit boards of directors. Most of these books and articles are written for the chief executive but many are also designed for board members themselves. Though the fact that boards of directors of nonprofit organizations are comprised of volunteers is acknowledged without argument, in practice the voluntary nature of boards is frequently overlooked. Are the successful practices of "volunteer management" applicable to boards of directors? Definitely, yes.

In Chapter 1 we examined the role of the board in developing the agency's philosophy of volunteerism, setting goals for volunteer involvement, and providing oversight of volunteer participation. In this chapter we are concerned about helping the board itself to be most effective as a group of active volunteers.

Recruitment and Job Descriptions   Recruitment of new board members can be done by following the model of how to recruit direct-service volunteers. Targeting potential sources of board members on the basis of special skills needed or type of representation sought is one way to find the right people. Similarly, having a written job description to show candidates will clarify what your organization expects of each individual board member. For board officers, additional job descriptions are needed to describe the requirements of each leadership position. By using job descriptions at the start of a board member's term, you are able to hold people to their commitments—whether this involves attendance at board meetings, follow-up activities during any given month, or a financial contribution.

There is a misconception that an organization's bylaws already provide job descriptions for board volunteers. The bylaws define *functions* and division of responsibility, but do not specify the practical, operational aspects of filling a board position. Also, the bylaws deal with functions that are continuous and timeless. Job descriptions, which should be updated regularly, apportion tasks necessary at any given point in time.

Be honest in writing board member job descriptions. Do not underestimate the time commitment involved in serving on the board. Remember to mention the work expected of board members in-between regular board meetings, including preparing in advance for the meetings and serving on sub-committees.

If you hope for—or expect—a financial contribution from every board member: say so. It is reasonable to ask the board to demonstrate their support of the organization with a donation. By openly stating this expectation, you can later solicit money from board volunteers more comfortably.

Developing Effective Working Relationships   Orientation and training are as important for board members as for any other volunteers. Regardless of the expertise for which the board member was recruited, no one is able to walk into a new situation and start being productive without learning the details of that particular situation. It is never insulting to offer board members the opportunity to learn about your organization—and someone who resents such an orientation session is probably an inappropriate recruit.

In your role as chief executive, you will be providing leadership to the board in ways that are very different from "supervising" in-house volunteers. One major difference is that the board is in charge; they have the final legal responsibility for the way your organization operates. Authority and power rests with them (even if some boards rarely exercise their power), including the right to hire and fire the chief executive. Even more sobering is the realization that the board of directors can legally make the decision to close the entire agency. Some boards make that decision by default, by not raising sufficient funds. But some boards make the active choice to end services, which may reflect the happy fact that those services may no longer be needed.

In order to make the best decisions for the agency, board members need your executive direction and advice, particularly in identifying the most pressing issues for the organization at any given time. Your most effective tool is persuasion—explaining and convincing the board of your point of view. You also need to provide resources with which board volunteers can accomplish tasks, explain how their work integrates with the rest of the agency's timetables, and also monitor that board work is getting done. All this requires setting a tone of harmony and energy—motivating board volunteers to give their utmost to the organization.

Periodically, it is nice to provide some recognition to board members for their hard work on behalf of the agency. It is too easy to become wrapped up in the problems of today and overlook the achievements of the past year. Again, because board members are volunteers, doing something to say thank you is always valid.

In some smaller (and even larger) organizations, board members become active in the daily work of providing services. In fact, the traditional way nonprofit organizations grow is that board members do *everything* in the beginning—from making policy to cleaning the office. Later, when funds are raised, a small corps of salaried staff takes over the operational side of the agency and the board redefines its role to goal and policy setting. This transition is not always accomplished without pain. It is hard for board members to relinquish control over activities they handled before the staff came on board. To some board volunteers, the hands-on work is more interesting than the policy decision-making and they prefer doing "practical" things.

On one level, it is healthy for board members to have some first-hand exposure to the work of the organization. It is questionable how a board can make decisions without some "reality testing" of the possible effect of certain actions. Also, needs assessment cannot be done objectively if all the data is funnelled through the CEO's perspective only.

You and the board must establish the boundary line between yourselves in your own way, based on the needs of the organization at this point in its history and on the personalities/ skills of the individuals involved. But it is important for you to recognize that roles must be *defined*. If some board members volunteer on-site on a regular schedule, then during those periods they should have a discrete job description and be "supervised" in much the same way any line volunteer would be. The dual demands of authority figure and direct worker should be separated as much as possible.

Sub-Committees of the Board

Depending on the type of subcommittees your board has designated, certain employees may be assigned as "liaison" staff to support the committees' work. This interface requires clarification of roles. For example, will the staff member be a voting member of the committee, or serve ex officio? For that matter, is the staff member expected to participate fully in discussions, or merely be present to act as a resource when requested?

The matter of who takes the minutes (both for the full board meeting and for sub-committees) deserves examination. Because this task seems clerical, it is common for volunteers to delegate this to salaried staff. Unfortunately, this serves to assign the "power of the pen" to the staff. Minutes present facts but also subjective interpretation of what was discussed. The written record of a meeting continues to influence the organization. Volunteers should retain the responsibility for reporting their own deliberations and decisions.

There are no clearly right or wrong ways to develop working relationships between the board and the staff. The variables of each organization must be considered. But the volunteer management principle of *defining* how the teamwork will operate is something that only you, as executive, can employ.

The Board Treasurer

The role of volunteer board treasurer is a special one and deserves attention here. The board of directors is responsible for the financial stewardship of the organization. The board member for whom this is a primary focus is the treasurer.

What this means in practice will change as your organization grows. If you have limited staff, the treasurer may actually keep the books. Or you may have this responsibility as part of your job description as executive director. Later, the agency may hire a bookkeeper. Eventually, there may be an entire accounting or finance department, with the previously-volunteer position of treasurer evolving into a salaried position within a board of trustees.

Until the organization has a full staff of employees working on finances, the board treasurer should be directly involved in monitoring the finances. This means physically coming into the agency regularly to provide oversight to the bookkeeper, co-signing checks (at least those above a board-agreed-upon amount), and generally assuring internal control. Even when there is a paid staff to handle such daily transactions, the treasurer still provides oversight. As long as the position is held by a volunteer, the treasurer should *present* the organization's financial statements to the board and be able to answer any questions related to them. The financial statements should explain in financial terms what you present in the narrative of your executive director's report.

The treasurer has the right—indeed the obligation—to *ask questions*. S/he watches what the organization is spending money on and thereby provides control for the board.

How the Director of Volunteers Can Help

The director of volunteers can be a real asset to you in building the board. Ironically, too few CEOs think of their director of volunteers in this context—yet who in the organization knows more about the demands of working with volunteers? Specifically, the director of volunteers can help you in the following ways:

- Because the director of volunteers is out in the community, s/he can be of assistance to the board nominating committee in suggesting possible candidates to join the board. Also, the director of volunteers can identify active, committed line volunteers who might be valuable board recruits because of their first-hand understanding of how the organization functions.

- The director of volunteers has great experience in writing volunteer job descriptions. Why not put this skill to work for the board?

- When designing an orientation for new board members, why start from scratch? The director of volunteers has already developed a curriculum, handouts, and perhaps even audio-visual aids that s/he uses to orient in-house volunteers. Most of this material will be equally applicable to board members and you can add whatever other information you need.

- The work contributed by board members should be included in any agency volunteer recognition event. To this end, the volunteer office could assist you in keeping records of board member activities, so that each board volunteer can be recognized for his/her special contributions. Any person who volunteers for the organization is a valuable resource—whether that voluntary service is given directly to your consumers or indirectly through policy making.

- Finally, board sub-committees may be composed entirely of board members or of a mixture of board members and non-board volunteers. The director of volunteers can certainly recruit non-board volunteers to join such committees and can train salaried staff to provide liaison support to these committees. Such support is another version of good staff/volunteer relationships.

There is no reason to think of board members and other organizational volunteers as completely different. Both groups are community members and, in their own ways, have clout.

Apart from the critical governance issues discussed in Chapter 1, there are a number of ways that board members can support the volunteer program.

How the Board Can Help the Volunteer Program

Depending on the stage of development of your program, and of its present staffing, there may be a need for a board sub-committee called something like the "Volunteer Resources Committee." It can help establish policy for in-house volunteers, assist in recruiting volunteers, and take an active role in evaluating the program.

Even without such a committee, individual board members can be called upon to make community presentations about the agency, perhaps combining appeals for funds and for volunteer participation. Members can be asked for referrals to sources of volunteers (such as an entree into a professional society, for example) or, particularly if a board member is an executive of a large business, asked to open channels for recruitment (such as placing a notice about volunteer opportunities into the corporate employee newsletter). Finally, board members should be invited to volunteer recognition events for the dual purpose of being thanked themselves and demonstrating the top-level support of agency decision-makers for frontline volunteers.

AUXILIARIES

There is no single model for how an auxiliary should support an organization. Quite diverse types of settings utilize auxiliaries. The list includes: hospitals, long-term care institutions, libraries, cultural arts groups, parks, and law enforcement agencies. Sometimes the group goes by a name such as "The Friends of _____" and may provide in-house volunteer work to the sponsoring organization on site. But most often an auxiliary's major purpose is to raise money.

Historically, auxiliaries were responsible for the funding of most of the institutions we hold dear. Also historically, auxiliaries were female organizations—frequently the wives of the staff or of the board members. In most cases, the auxilians raised the money and turned it over to the decision-makers of the sponsor group. In other cases, the auxilians participated in determining how the money would be spent. These two approaches still exist today. In some organizations, the president of the auxiliary has a seat on the board of directors.

For the purposes of this book, what is important about auxiliaries is to recognize their volunteer nature and to analyze whether you, as executive, have created the best working environment. You should assess:

1. Is the interrelationship of the auxiliary and your agency clearly defined? Is the auxiliary autonomous or do you, as sponsor, have some formal decision-making role to play in its governance?

2. Who are the members of the auxiliary? What are the criteria for joining and are new members recruited with these criteria in mind? Does the auxiliary perpetuate exclusionary practices such as limiting membership only to women, to people able to pay membership dues, or other rules? If so, are these discriminatory practices justifiable?

3. Is the auxiliary still strong or is it a remnant of its old self from years ago, with members aging fast and no longer able to give or generate financial contributions comparable to those in the past?

4. Is there an actual or implied hierarchy in which the auxiliary has more status than the in-house volunteers?

5. What is the relationship between the auxiliary officers and the director of volunteers? Is there a direct line of authority (in what direction)? Why or why not? (Similarly, is there a clear relationship between the auxiliary and the development office?)

6. Does the auxiliary president expect and receive direct communication with you as CEO? Why or why not?

7. Do you receive regular reports from the auxiliary on all aspects of its operation, including membership statistics and financial statements?

8. If the auxiliary is not self-incorporated, what is the parent organization's responsibility/liability in terms of tax reporting, auditing, etc.? To whom do the bank accounts really belong?

As mentioned earlier, if your organization is partnering or merging with another agency or facility, does this affect two or more friends groups? The politics of mergers are delicate in the best of cases, so it is important to consider all the affected constituents. There are no standard ways to assure the success of combined or separate-but-equal auxiliaries, but it is always a mistake to assume unquestioned loyalty, especially to a redesigned institution. Invite supporter group leaders to develop the best strategies with you and they will develop ownership of the process.

Interrelationships

This is a matter of situational management. If you are working with a strong, viable auxiliary that raises lots of money for your organization, certain ways of interacting will derive from the situation. Also, if the auxiliary is clearly focused solely on fundraising, it is easy to draw the line between auxilian volunteers and in-house, direct service volunteers. In fact, in that type of separation, any auxilian who *also* wants to become involved in direct service should be interviewed and placed into a volunteer assignment through the volunteer program office, as would any other non-auxilian volunteer. When working on-site, that person would be a "patient escort," "docent," "clerical aide," or whatever volunteer title applies. Her or his additional role as an "auxilian" would not affect the in-house volunteer function.

In some facilities, the auxiliary runs the in-house volunteer program. This may be quite workable but avoid the requirement that anyone who wants to volunteer has to *join* the auxiliary. This is one way to perpetuate discrimination and outmoded tradition, especially if there are special criteria for becoming an auxiliary member. Perhaps more importantly, few auxiliaries are able to accommodate the type of volunteer who wants to come in for one month to re-catalog your library or who is on-call to help with press releases when needed. These types of assignments are rarely filled by people seeking to join the auxiliary or wanting the additional social aspects of group activities.

As CEO, you can establish guidelines to assure that any qualified person wanting to offer volunteer help is encouraged to apply, rather than being turned down at the first contact because s/he does not qualify as an "auxilian."

If your friends group organizes major revenue-producing events on behalf of your agency, how do these activities mesh with the projected plans of your development staff or special events staff? Are plans determined mutually in advance? Who has final say over theme, ticket prices, and other elements of the event which might reflect on your organization's public image? Who keeps the records and submits reports (and to whom)? Who thinks about insurance and other legal issues? Who sends thank you notes when an event is over? Unless you clarify these types of questions in advance, you may someday discover that this year's auxiliary leaders have a very different point of view about what to do (in your agency's name) than you ever anticipated.

The real challenge to you as executive is the situation in which you have a weak auxiliary and a growing, vital volunteer program. You will have to examine the possible risks involved in placing the auxiliary under the jurisdiction of the volunteer office or the development office in an effort either to retire the group or to build it up again.

Facilities in inner city areas have in recent years seen a trend in auxiliaries whose members never set foot in the actual agency—who prefer, in fact, to keep several miles between themselves and the concrete reality of the problems the facility is trying to address. Again, some of these volunteer groups are successful in raising a great deal of money through suburban "thrift" shops, debutante balls, etc. and receive publicity and status for their efforts. This fundraising is vital and should not be denigrated because the volunteers disassociate themselves from the recipients of service. However, it is only fair to give comparable credit to those volunteers who, though not wealthy contributors, are willing to come on site, roll up their sleeves and work directly with daily service delivery. This type of personal involvement deserves some status, too.

Given today's volunteerism climate, the concept of an auxiliary only makes sense if you feel that you want to maintain a fundraising group with a sense of unity. The social aspects of auxiliaries are indeed important to accomplishing the work, for many fundraising events require long hours of service and it is much more pleasant to volunteer in the company of friends. But you should expect the auxiliary to set goals, submit reports, and make a visible contribution.

It is legitimate to question low performance. After all, the auxiliary only exists to support your agency, even if the members have evolved an "us and them" mentality. Unfortunately, because some auxilians are wealthy or influential, executives may be reluctant to "make waves" by challenging the status quo. Further complicating this may be discomfort at seeming to criticize older women. The real problem in too many cases is that auxilians were left to their own devices years ago and it is difficult to recapture a good working relationship after so much neglect.

As the top administrator, you establish the standards. Auxilian volunteers deserve to know how they can be of most help, just as other types of volunteers should be recognized for their equally vital contributions to the organization. Ultimately it is the agency's image in the community that is most affected if an auxiliary or friends group is allowed to atrophy.

ADVISORY COUNCILS

As with boards of directors and auxiliaries, advisory councils are special categories of volunteers with direct relationship to you as the CEO. If you are heading a unit of government, you may be working with a legally mandated advisory council including some or all members designated by virtue of their public positions or appointed by political leaders. Or you may have a council voluntarily established by your agency to gain more community input. Either way, members of your advisory council will respond most productively to motivating behavior on your part.

Clear expectations are imperative. Just because you have an "advisory" council does not mean that anyone has promised to use the advice given! Take the time to define exactly what the role of the advisory group is—and what it is not. Do not imply power when there is none. Most advisory groups have an impact through influence and persuasion, rather than through decision-making authority.

For this reason, it is good to avoid the use of the word "board" in relation to advisors. When someone joins a group called the "Advisory Board," there may be an implication of authority well beyond anything intended. Designations such as "Advisory Council" or "Community Representative Task Force" are more accurate.

Using the Principles of Volunteer Management

Recruitment of members onto an advisory council should be done with the same consideration as the recruitment of any other volunteers. Criteria for membership should be determined and a process instituted for interviewing, screening and orienting candidates and new members. Clarify whether a person serves as an advisor because of her or his personal credentials or by virtue of a position s/he holds. If the latter, does the individual automatically resign if s/he changes jobs? A written job description for each member, with additional tasks for council officers, is also a critical tool. Be sure to indicate terms of office or else you may imply that advisors serve forever. The director of volunteers can be of assistance to you in this process, just as described in working effectively with the board of directors.

Getting the Best Advice

If you have an advisory council, utilize it. People who have volunteered prefer to be active than to see their names used on letterhead for political clout, without having had any input into what the organization is doing. (Otherwise put together an "Honorary Circle of Support" and be open about wanting to use influential names only.)

One of the obstacles to genuine involvement of advisory councils is the feeling that the only way to activate them is to call a group meeting. Ironically, full council meetings tend to work contrary to the goal of getting advice. Most advisors have been recruited because they "represent" a specific constituency: an ethnic group, neighborhood, profession, funding source, etc. In a group meeting, these very different people attempt to reach consensus on issues. In the process of reaching consensus, special interest, minority opinions are overlooked or played down. But, as executive, it is often those very minority opinions that you most wanted advice about!

There are two ways to counteract this tendency to make the advisory council function as a group. One is to ask advisor volunteers to provide service in two distinct ways: participate in one or two group meetings of the full advisory council per year, and also spend a few hours consulting with you one-to-one. Sometimes what you need is the perspective of someone with a very specific point of view. You can best gain this information individually—group meetings will dilute the opinions of any one particular advisor.

The other way to assure the benefit of many diverse points of view is to make sure advisory council meetings never take a vote. Taking a vote implies that the council can make policy, which it cannot, so allowing the majority to express only one opinion is misleading anyway. Instead of trying to distill all members' perspectives into one, try the following:

—get the council to list all the *pros and cons* of any idea under discussion;

—have the group generate a list of all the *questions* they can think of in reaction to a particular issue (sometimes a good question is more valuable than a lengthy statement of opinion);

—ask for the minutes to reflect the *"minority opinion,"* just as the Supreme Court will publish the perspective of those judges who disagree with the ruling of the Court;

—ask council members to suggest community *resources* that might assist with a particular project.

This type of approach gives you a great deal of advice that you can use and also makes advisor volunteers feel recognized for their input.

If your advisory council has been selected for its high degree of professional expertise, you may occasionally want the group to give you the benefit of their specific knowledge and "instruct" you on what course of action to take. In such special cases, taking a vote may be desirable. But differentiate between those situations in which you want general advice and those in which you are, in essence, delegating decision making. Otherwise, the advisors will assume that all their input carries the weight of giving instructions, which is probably not the case.

You do not have to establish an advisory body as a standing committee. In fact, it is sometimes most useful to recruit advisors for an ad hoc, time-limited task force focused on one particular need for expertise. Tasks could range from advising on site selection for a new building to the design of an evaluation study.

Finally, be sure everyone understands the difference between the roles of any advisory council and the organization's board of directors. For example, does the advisory council advise you, as administrator, or the board, as governors? Lines of authority can quickly become blurred, especially if you routinely encourage volunteers such as past board presidents to continue their service to your agency by joining the advisory council. Because you are the one person with a leadership role in both groups, you can demonstrate the differences between them by the way you plan each set of agendas, deliver reports to each group, and so on.

LEGAL ISSUES

Some of the issues that arise from the involvement of volunteers relate to questions of law. There are real legal concerns regarding the liability of and for volunteers, while other issues are quasi-legal in nature. Because of the seriousness of such questions, they require executive involvement.

Control

Whether stated directly or not, many of the questions asked about volunteers center on the concern for control. Legitimately, administrators want to be confident that their staff members provide services in accordance with the policies of the organization. Such confidence is bolstered by the belief that there is a clearly understood system of rewards for doing the job right and consequences for doing it wrong.

When managing employees, "rewards" available include a pay raise, a promotion, more vacation time, or some other tangible demonstration of positive recognition. "Consequences" are also tangible and range from withholding a pay raise to the ultimate threat of termination of employment. In the last analysis, both top executives and line workers feel that it is the threat of being fired—the mere possibility of it—that keeps employees "in line."

This is the crux of the debate about volunteers and control. What threat can an organization hold over the head of a volunteer that is as controlling as losing one's income?

But this question reflects a number of interesting attitudes. First, it indicates the managerial perspective that the threat of punishment is the best motivator for generating good work. Second, it confuses the available punishment with a guarantee of *prevention* of some unwanted behavior. And third, it neglects the important fact that the initial reasons for why the volunteer chose to come to the agency had nothing to do with a salary.

Managerially, it is more effective to govern through rewards than through negative consequences. Recognizing and visibly showing appreciation for work done right is far more motivating to everyone on staff than responding only to negative acts. Clearly, it is possible to reward volunteers in a variety of tangible ways similar to recognition of employees, including promotion to more responsible assignments.

For some paid workers, the fear of being fired or even of a lesser consequence will indeed stop them from doing something wrong. But the person who no longer cares about the agency, is too weak to resist temptation, or believes him/herself clever enough to avoid detection will act despite any threat to his/her job. Also, many acts you as an administrator may consider "wrong," may be done in innocence, out of ignorance, or through strong personal convictions that happen to differ from the agency position. It is therefore a delusion to think that it is possible to prevent wrong doing through the threat of punishment.

The best way to feel confident about control of the organization's service providers is to start with careful screening of employees—and volunteers—at the time they apply to the organization. This includes clarifying expectations on both sides, particularly about any areas of service that might involve philosophic points of view. Another tool to assure compliance with agency rules is training. Both employees and volunteers deserve full instruction on how to do their jobs in the best way. This whole process is then reinforced by supervision and evaluation, including positive recognition for doing the job well. Even with this approach, prevention of problems cannot be guaranteed, but the likelihood of wrong doing is not determined by who receives a salary and who does not.

Finally, since money is not the reason why volunteers joined your organization in the first place, why should anyone miss having the control tool of threatening to take away money? If a volunteer cares a great deal about participating in your organization, then the most effective "threat" would be to no longer allow the person to volunteer. Yes, this means it is possible to "fire" a volunteer. The punishment is not losing an income, it is losing the chance to be involved.

Some administrators harbor the nightmare that if they tried to fire a volunteer, that person would simply say: "You can't tell me to leave; I'm a volunteer." First, the chances of this happening are so remote that it should never stop you from terminating a volunteer. The person who tries to argue with you probably has some other problem, be it an ax to grind or mental illness. Most healthy people would never stay in a place where they were no longer wanted. Second, from a legal standpoint, you do indeed have the right to designate who will be an agent of your organization—whether paid or not. Under any circumstance, document the reasons for firing the volunteer, just as you would do with an employee.

In short, control is really not dependent upon paying a salary. Your best management approach for paid staff and volunteers alike is to motivate through approval.

Confidentiality

The subject of confidentiality is closely linked to control and, in fact, is often raised as a smokescreen to hide the underlying fear that volunteers are uncontrollable. Confidentiality is an important and serious issue, but it is a *training* issue, not one tied to salaried versus voluntary employment.

Volunteers should be screened and trained to understand the meaning of client confidentiality and the necessity of maintaining it. In fact, violation of confidentiality should be stated as cause for immediate dismissal. However, whether or not a person gossips has nothing whatsoever to do with level of pay. Volunteers are no more prone to speak about a case outside of the agency than are salaried staff. In fact, the probability may even be less. Volunteers rarely discuss their volunteer experiences with their friends (one of the reasons why so many members of the public harbor the mistaken belief that no one volunteers any more!), while salaried staff are more likely to describe the happenings of their work week in a social context. This is also due to the fact that volunteers come in contact with clients for a few hours a week, while employees spend forty hours with the agency's consumers. So who has more to talk about?

Any agent of the organization deserves to have access to whatever records or information are necessary in order to accomplish her/his assigned tasks. Conversely, this means that no one should be allowed to peruse records not relevant to an assigned case or to "eavesdrop" on other workers' activities. Both of these principles should apply equally to employees and volunteers. You do not give any and all employees access to client records. For example, the maintenance department would hardly have a good reason to read counseling records. Just as you are able to differentiate which employees may be given confidential information, you can select which volunteers require such data to complete their assignments.

If a volunteer is given a job to do that involves a particular client, it undercuts all chance for success to deny that volunteer access to the necessary background information. Much of this stems from suspicion that somehow the volunteer is "dabbling" in providing service and only the serious (i.e., salaried) worker should know the full story. Remember that this book makes the assumption that you have made sure all volunteers are appropriately selected and matched only to assignments that they are capable of fulfilling.

If you still have some doubts, ask the client directly for permission to reveal records to the volunteer. However you chose to handle this issue, the end result must be that you stand behind the volunteer as a legitimate representative of your organization.

Questions of Law   *At various points in this book, I have indicated issues that may require seeking the advice of your organization's lawyer, accountant, or other expert consultants. We have reached a subject for which I decided to practice what I preach! The following pages were written by Jeffrey D. Kahn, Esq., Assistant General Counsel for The Children's Hospital of Philadelphia and frequent collaborator on Energize, Inc. projects. Jeffrey has long been interested in legal issues related to volunteers. He wrote the original version of this chapter and has written other articles and publications about volunteerism. In 1992, Jeffrey co-authored the guidebook,* Managing Legal Liability and Insurance for Corporate Volunteer Programs *(Nonprofit Risk Management Center).*

The management of volunteers presents many of the same legal issues as the management of employees: What laws regulate the conduct of the organization in setting the parameters of the work to be done and the selection and supervision of the people to do the work? How should your program operate so that it minimizes liability while accomplishing its mission? Volunteers, like employees, can be accidentally injured or accidentally cause some injury to others while carrying out their duties. The leaders of an organization need to understand these potential liabilities and take steps to minimize the organization's exposure, such as practicing good risk management and maintaining insurance, just as is done with respect to employees.

The following pages will articulate some of the questions—and not even all of the questions—you might consider and raise with your organization's lawyers as your organization examines the management of its volunteer program. The purpose here is not to provide any professional advice. Only a full discussion with your attorney will give you specific information about the federal, state and local laws that apply to your program. An attorney who knows your organization can help you develop steps to minimize your legal exposure.

In recent years, there has been a growing body of literature about the legal and insurance issues relating to the management of volunteers. Some of these materials are included in the bibliography in Appendix B. While this chapter notes some of the general legal issues, the excellent materials that now exist (and that did not exist as recently as five years ago) provide the best sources for executives to explore these issues in more depth.

Keep in mind that discussions of potential legal problems always center on "worst case" scenarios. As you weigh your options for the utilization of volunteers, objectively analyze the range of difficult situations that could occur, and the likelihood of their occurrence. Consider each volunteer assignment category separately. Are the possible problems (and their potential cost) so great that they begin to offset the benefits your organization derives from various volunteer activities? In most cases you will probably conclude that the net effect of volunteer involvement is positive enough to justify working with volunteers, though you might take precautions to prevent the occurrence of any "worst case" situation.

Just as you do not allow complex potential legal difficulties to inhibit you from hiring salaried personnel, the existence of similar legal questions should not become a roadblock to the utilization of volunteers.

The Employer/ Employee Relationship   Earlier in this book we suggested that you consider volunteers as your nonsalaried personnel department. That characterization is useful in thinking about legal issues as well as managerial ones.

Any discussion of legal issues involving "volunteers" would be much simpler if there were a single, neat legal definition of a "volunteer" that works across the board. Unfortunately, many of the legal issues involving volunteers involve the question of whether laws designed to apply to "employees" also apply to volunteers. However, there is not even a single definition of "employee" that can be used to simplify the discussion. For each issue, one must examine the definitions of employee and employer used in the legal sources and decide whether they apply to volunteers. For example, an individual might be considered an employee for purposes of a state workers compensation statute even though no salary is paid because the person receives significant in-kind compensation. The same individual might not be covered by the state's anti-discrimination law because no salary is paid.

Employment Law Issues   Issues of whether a volunteer fits within the legal definitions of employee arise most prominently in thinking about the application of labor and employment laws to volunteers. Even some laws that would seem to have no application to volunteers, such as the Fair Labor Standards Act, might in fact have some relevance.

Laws prohibiting employment discrimination against members of protected classes generally do not apply to volunteers. Most courts that have analyzed these laws have concluded that volunteers normally are not included in the definition of "employee." However, as noted above, the scope of these laws may vary, especially at the state and local level. Some such laws may indeed protect volunteers, which means that a volunteer might bring an action alleging discrimination. It is probably safest—and good policy—to use the same type of standards you have for avoiding discrimination in hiring and firing employees in the management of volunteers. The questions that are irrelevant and improper to ask in interviewing a prospective employee do not become acceptable when the person applying for a position is a prospective volunteer. Similarly, questions of access for disabled persons may arise under the Americans with Disabilities Act in connection with volunteers, just as such issues arise with employees, clients, visitors, and other persons.

You should also use care in delineating categories of work to be performed by volunteers and employees. Having the same position filled by some people who are volunteers and others who are paid employees may raise real legal concerns. First, if the employees in question are members of a union, you could be in violation of a union contract if volunteers are used to "replace" union members. Second, the Fair Labor Standards Act, which sets minimum wage standards and is designed to prevent exploitation of certain categories of workers by certain types of employers, may prohibit an arrangement in which employees and volunteers do similar tasks in the same organization.

That Act may also raise questions about employees who wish to volunteer for the organization on their own time. You should be careful to ensure that such dedicated employees are doing volunteer work that is wholly unrelated to their normal paid work, and that such volunteering is clearly "voluntary." While the law is not entirely clear, at this point, the best advice would be to use the following guidelines:

1. Be sure that no pressure—overt or implied—is given to make an employee feel that extra time is "expected." It should be a free choice to volunteer.

2. Insist that the employee "apply" for a volunteer position, filling out a volunteer application form and going through the volunteer office for placement. The employee should sign in and out on the volunteer attendance form, separate from any employee time logs.

3. The assignment the volunteer carries should be demonstrably different from the job description of the person's salaried position.

Liability for Acts of Volunteers

In the past, most nonprofit organizations were not liable for harm caused by anyone working for the organization, whether salaried or not, but were protected by a legal doctrine called "charitable immunity." Most states have now abolished this shield from liability, and nonprofit organizations are now liable for damage caused by any of the organization's workers, just as any business would be liable.

There is a general legal principle that a master is liable for injuries caused by his or her servant during the servant's performance of his or her work. Courts apply this doctrine (called *respondeat superior*) to employers and hold them fully liable for damage caused by an employee on the job. A number of courts have also applied this doctrine to instances in which a volunteer caused the damage.

In order for your organization to be liable for damage caused by a volunteer, three conditions must be met:

—the volunteer must have negligently or intentionally caused the damage;

—the volunteer must have been performing his or her assigned work at the time of the accident;

—the volunteer must have been a "servant" of the organization, that is, within the control of the organization.

All three of these requirements involve complex legal concepts which vary from state to state, and which your lawyer can define more fully. The bottom line, however, is that in most states your organization would be fully liable for any harm caused by a volunteer participating in a structured volunteer program, regardless of how careful your management or supervision.

An organization may also have direct liability for failing to take proper steps to supervise or support volunteers, if the organization itself is "negligent" in these activities and some harm ensues. There are also circumstances in which a volunteer will be considered the "agent" of an organization with the power to bind the organization to legal obligations.

While the above summary of the law may surprise some readers, this is no different than the law for salaried employees. Rather than

Anticipating Potential Liability

risk having to pay the full cost of damage accidentally caused by a volunteer (such damages awarded by a court can be considerable), most employers of salaried and nonsalaried servants take two types of precautions. First, they engage in risk management to help reduce the chance of accidents ever occurring. Second, they purchase insurance that will pay for the damage in the event an accident does occur.

Your organization probably practices some degree of risk management already. For example, you may require employees or volunteers to have certain experience or training before performing specific tasks. Requiring that a volunteer have a lifesaving certificate before being assigned to conduct a swimming program is a form of risk management, since certified lifeguards are more apt to take the necessary safety measures than those without such formal training. Risk management involves anticipating the most likely ways a volunteer could accidentally cause damage, and then devising reasonable and cost-effective ways to reduce the likelihood of these accidents. Preventive techniques include requiring special training or education of volunteers, ensuring proper supervision of volunteers, and screening volunteers for certain personality traits (responsibility, maturity, ability to handle stress, etc.).

While the requirement that a volunteer lifeguard have a lifesaving certificate is an easy form of pre-employment screening, other screening issues may raise more complex concerns. If the volunteer will be working with a vulnerable population, such as children, a child abuse screening may be in order (or even legally required) to prevent the organization from placing clients at risk. See the excellent publications, *Staff Screening Tool Kit* and *Child Abuse Prevention Primer*, listed in the bibliography, for a full discussion of these issues. Other organizations may feel the need to screen certain categories of volunteers to be sure that they do not carry infections such as HIV or tuberculosis. Again, this raises serious legal issues. Use the guidelines developed for screening employees to decide how—and whether—to perform health screening on volunteers.

One important risk management tool is the clear communication of expectations and responsibilities of both the volunteer and the organization. Written job descriptions are therefore useful in describing the duties and qualifications of the volunteer and the support the volunteer will receive. Some organizations go further and ask volunteers to sign formal contracts. A contract for the provision of volunteer services, if it is to be enforceable, must still meet the usual requirements for what makes a valid contract, including the requirement that each side must receive some benefit. Contracts are often used to provide remedies in case of a breach, but that may be inappropriate in situations involving volunteers. A written job description may accomplish the same purposes of memorializing each side's obligations and the necessary qualifications of the volunteer.

It is of course essential that you have some liability insurance to cover damage caused by volunteers, and you should check to see what your current policy covers. It is important that your insurance *explicitly* covers damage caused by volunteers. Since insurance brokers and carriers may be unfamiliar with volunteer programs (and may even harbor the prejudice that volunteers are especially risky), you should be ready to explain the steps your organization takes to adequately train and supervise volunteers. With volunteers, as with salaried employees, you will need to weigh the cost of insuring certain activities against the benefits you derive from these activities.

Volunteers' Personal Liability

In addition to the liability of the organization for harm caused by volunteers, the volunteers themselves may have personal liability. The basis of the volunteer's liability would be the same as that of an employee: negligence or some other breach of a prevailing standard of care or rule of law.

Recently, many states have adopted laws that protect volunteers personally from liability, so long as the volunteer was not acting maliciously or in bad faith. The terms of these laws vary considerably. It is also now possible to purchase insurance at a relatively modest cost to protect volunteers themselves in cases of alleged personal liability, and your organization may wish to investigate such insurance on behalf of its volunteers.

The reality in most cases is that, regardless of the volunteer's possible personal exposure, an injured party will look to the organization as the "deep pocket" from whom payment will be demanded. Your organization will usually want to defend a lawsuit on behalf of both the organization and the volunteer, just as you would do if an employee were sued along with the organization.

Liability for Injuries to Volunteers

A volunteer who gets injured may attempt to recover medical or other costs from the organization. Whether the volunteer is entitled to such compensation depends on the circumstances surrounding the accident and whether the organization or any of its servants acted in a negligent manner. This situation is, for legal purposes, similar to that in which a client or other third party is injured by the volunteer. Once again, you should check to see if your insurance covers this situation. In some states, certain categories of volunteers are covered under workers compensation laws, though in most cases such laws do not apply to volunteers. Again, check with your lawyer to find out about the specific requirements of your state's law.

One way to reduce the chances of your organization being sued for injury suffered by a volunteer is to have the volunteer sign a waiver of liability. In consulting with your lawyer about the usefulness of a liability waiver, you should realize that such waivers are often not as effective as they might seem. A waiver only operates as a bar to legal action if it can be shown that the signer fully understood the risk involved and the meaning of the waiver, and signed it voluntarily. Even so, a waiver may be useful because it provides an opportunity to discuss possible risks with the volunteers, and because some volunteers will honor the waiver agreement and not sue in the event of injury.

The volunteer who gets injured may have other sources of compensation, such as personal insurance, which would make it unnecessary to proceed against your organization. However, you may still want to provide insurance coverage to volunteers. Such insurance often provides for payment only in "excess" of other coverage available.

Car and Drivers Insurance   If volunteer assignments involve driving a motor vehicle, be sure to check appropriate insurance coverage. Though the specific concerns may be affected by whether the volunteers are authorized to drive an agency car or van, or utilize their private vehicles, liability is an issue in both cases.

Board Member Indemnification   Members of your board of directors can be liable for various "errors" or "omissions" committed in the line of decision making for the organization. In recognition of this, many organizations have purchased insurance to protect their board in case the individual members are named in a suit. Under such insurance, the insurer will usually cover the costs of any lawsuit and will pay any damages awarded, within agreed-upon limits. The recent laws protecting volunteers from personal liability also apply to board members. These laws vary from state to state. You should check on when board members can be sued in your state, and should investigate insurance options.

Resolve Concerns   All of these legal issues raise complex questions which an attorney can help you fully understand and resolve. Such consultation should help you to anticipate possible legal problems before they arise and to strengthen the way your organization involves volunteers. The resources in the bibliography may help you define your questions and clarify your thinking on particular legal and insurance issues.

EVALUATION OF VOLUNTEER IMPACT

Because you expend time, money and other resources on the involvement of volunteers, it is clearly good management practice to evaluate whether this expense is worth it. It also should be of interest to assess what volunteers accomplish and how well they do it. In fact, this assessment is of equal interest to the volunteers themselves, since no one wants to give time to do something that has no impact.

Some agencies routinely overlook the volunteer component when they do an internal evaluation study. As CEO, you can see to it that services provided by volunteers are evaluated with the same concern as those delivered by employees.

What to Assess

One of the most uncreative—and unhelpful—questions posed to volunteer program leaders is: "How many volunteers do we have and how many hours did they give us this year?" Unfortunately, this is too often the extent of program "evaluation" for the volunteer component. A tally of hours served without analysis of what was accomplished and how well it was done is not worth compiling. It is a left-handed compliment to assume that somehow the importance of volunteer involvement is self-evident. It is up to the top executive to require some demonstration of the value of volunteers.

One of the problems in evaluating volunteer achievement is that certain types of volunteer assignments require services that are described in terms of their quality, rather than their quantity. Indeed, the titles given to some of these assignments reflect the inherent "how-can-we-ever-measure-this?" aspect of the work: "friendly" visitor; Big "Brother"; victim "support" counselor. In reality, it is quite possible to determine some identifiable bench-marks of achievement, regardless of the assignment. Such indica-tors may be a bit subjective, but both the recipient and the giver of service should be able to point to successes such as: the client makes a point of asking the volunteer's advice on something; the teenager goes to school regularly for two months; the patient's family identifies an increase in morale.

It is equally difficult to evaluate the efforts of salaried staff on services designed to affect the "quality of life" for recipients. Accountability and evaluation are nevertheless sought after by all types of agencies, so the challenge of finding ways to assess the impact of volunteer efforts may have implications for other ser-vice evaluation as well.

If measurable goals and objectives are articulated for the volunteer program at the start of the period under evaluation, it will obviously be possible to ask whether these were met. An evaluation (probably annual) should analyze performance in sev-eral areas:

1. The actual quantity and quality of the work done by vol-unteers—preferably in each assignment category.

2. The accomplishments of the volunteer management team, including such overview questions as the demo-graphic makeup of the volunteer corps, number and type of recruitment outreach efforts, etc.

3. The type and degree of service provided to employees by volunteers and/or the volunteer program office.

4. The benefits to the organization as a whole from volun-teer involvement.

Some of the questions that could be asked to assess the contribution of volunteers in a given period are similar to those that would be asked about the work of salaried staff. In addition, consider some of the following approaches to identifying the value of volunteers:

—Have our consumers expressed any awareness of, appreciation for, or comments about volunteers here?

—What were we able to do more of this year than last because of the extra help from volunteers?

—What did volunteers free staff to do?

—What were we able to innovate or experiment with this year because volunteers agreed to test something new?

—In which volunteer assignments did we have the most turnover and why? Which assignments are the most popular with volunteers and why?

—Has our public relations or image changed and can we trace any of this change to the impact of volunteers?

—Is our volunteer corps representative of the community we serve?

—Have members of the salaried staff visibly developed their supervisory skills as a result of working with volunteers?

These are the kinds of questions that will provide information immediately translatable into management decisions. The data gathered can be used to uncover training needs, recruitment strategies, service deserving recognition, and other things to do.

Comparisons

There is one danger worth mentioning. Be cautious of drawing comparisons between the work of volunteers and that of employees. As you are already aware, this book recommends making sure that the job descriptions of volunteers differ tangibly from those of employees. If you follow this advice, it will always be clear that you are evaluating each group separately, based on the different assignments they are each handling.

However, we have also already identified one major reason

why volunteers are threatening to salaried staff: the fear that, if volunteers do well, it will raise questions about the role played by employees. When reporting the results of any evaluation, therefore, it is helpful to praise the good work of both groups— and also to indicate areas of weakness/need for improvement of both groups.

At times there are reasons to do some comparing between the service provided solely by paid staff and the service provided by a combination of effort by employees and volunteers. This is important if you are trying, for example, to measure the impact of one-to-one volunteers assisting juvenile probationers. One way to do the measuring would be to compare the rate of recidivism of probationers without an adult volunteer friend to those with a volunteer. While this is a very reasonable evaluation approach, recognize that it could *imply* something about the abilities of the various probation officers, too. Here is an excellent example of how the wording of the final evaluation report can help or hurt volunteer/employee relationships.

Ongoing Assessment: Volunteer Program Reports Apart from an annual or periodic evaluation of the volunteer program, you should be looking for indicators all year round of whether volunteers are being effective—and whether your organization is providing the most supportive working environment for volunteers.

This means requiring reports from the director of volunteers with the same frequency as you require them from other department heads, probably monthly. The data in these reports will be compiled from statistics being maintained in the volunteer office, but also from reports submitted to the director of volunteers by the various departments in which volunteers operate. You can also ask each department to include the accomplishments of volunteers in their unit directly to you within their monthly report. (This is another way to demonstrate that you are interested.)

Among the things to look for in regular reports are such data as the rate of turnover in specific assignment categories, accomplishments of short-term versus long-term volunteers, and assignments that have been vacant for an unusually long time.

The data may alert you to trouble spots. If turnover seems to occur monthly in a particular unit, perhaps there is a problem with the supervisory staff or the physical environment there.

As with all data, the numbers alone do not tell the whole story. Some statistics reflect normal variables in the operation of a volunteer program, such as anticipated high rates of turnover in a particular month (such as students leaving in June). Vacancies may demonstrate the careful screening being done by the director of volunteers, who is willing to allow vacancies for a time rather than to fill a slot with inappropriate volunteers. See if the report includes information on recruitment efforts focused on the unfilled assignment categories and if the number of screening interviews of applicants is higher than the number of new volunteers actually brought on board.

The director of volunteers also has the responsibility of giving you information about volunteers that is useful to you in your work as executive. At any given time, you should know the answers to the following questions:

—What is the "profile" of the volunteers in your facility? Specifically:
    —what is the range of ages represented?
    —the percentage of men and women?
    —their racial distribution?
    —the neighborhoods they represent?

—*Exactly* what do volunteers do?

—Do they perform these roles successfully? (By what criteria?)

—Which units in the agency do not utilize volunteers? Why not?

—Where is the highest turnover of volunteers, and why?

—How many public relations and community contacts are made weekly by the Volunteer Department, with which organizations or individuals, and with what results?

—What suggestions or observations are being made by volunteers that might be useful to agency management?

If the director of volunteers is not already supplying you with this type of data, ask for it. Think about how much more useful such data is than the so-called bottom line figure of "how many volunteers do we have?"

Computerizing

As you computerize your organization's records, plan to include the volunteer office's records as well. But be sure that your computer programmers talk with the director of volunteers before designing the software for volunteer records. Time and again colleagues call me in despair at the attitude of management information system staff that volunteer program management data is nothing more than a glorified "address list" that can be added on to some fundraising or accounting software with only a few modifications. The recordkeeping needs of the volunteer office are rather complex, including matching people to assignments and coordinating schedules that change each day.

In recent years, as desktop computers proliferate and even the smallest of agencies have computerized, software developed specifically for volunteer management has come on the market. Give some consideration to such a purchase, even if you want to integrate all the files of your agency into one computer system. The computer needs of your development office or your casework supervisors are simply not the same as the needs of the volunteer office. On a daily basis, the director of volunteers handles fluid data that changes with the current schedules and activities of volunteers. The available off-the-shelf programs for volunteer recordkeeping are comparatively low cost, especially compared to developing your own software, and generally better. The money spent on the right software will be an investment in improved ability to coordinate volunteers.

For large institutions and as the technology becomes more accessible to smaller agencies, you can consider going on-line with an interactive system. This allows volunteers to log in daily, immediately updating service records and entering information on their activities. Cyberspace also holds amazing possibilities for future methods of keeping in contact with off-site volunteers via e-mail, Web sites, and other virtual "staff meeting" forums.

Though it is reasonably obvious, it does not hurt to point out that the evaluation of the volunteer pro- gram is not the same thing as an **Evaluating the Director of Volunteers**

evaluation of your director of volunteers. You are justified in assessing the competence and achievements of the director of volunteers by examining the way in which the volunteer program is managed, but the achievements of the *volunteers* themselves are not necessarily the reflection—nor the fault—of the leader of the program.

A great deal depends on your expectations of what the position of director of volunteers means to your agency. If you set your sights low and only want a volunteer program "main- tained," then you do not need much in the way of creativity or vision from your director of volunteers. If you recognize the potential of this component of your service delivery, you will want the leader to be a full participatory member of your admin- istrative team.

Leland Kaiser, an authority in hospital management, has an interesting point of view about what an executive should expect from any department head. He challenges CEOs to require every department head, on an annual basis, to report on the major trends and issues affecting his/her area of specialty. Kaiser's point is that leadership involves not only day-to-day management, but also continuing education about developments in the outside world that will impact on your operations.

You should hold the director of volunteers responsible for keeping informed about volunteerism in general. S/he is, as already indicated, your in-house expert on volunteers. Is s/he truly aware of what is happening with citizen participation in other settings? Can s/he express long-range goals for the volun- teer program and predict changes that will occur in the future? Is s/he aware of trends in your organization's specific field (health care, recreation, child welfare, etc.) and how these might affect your needs for volunteer involvement in the future?

Individual Volunteer Evaluations
Yes, it is legitimate and reasonable to evaluate the individual performance of volunteers—providing that volunteers know in advance that there will be periodic assessment, that it is done equitably for all volunteers, and that it is based on having told each volunteer what was expected from him or her in the first place (the job description). In fairness, the evaluation should be a two-way process, also allowing the volunteer the chance to give feedback on the support received from the organization.

It is more than semantics to call the volunteer evaluation a "progress report" or "future action plan." This sounds less judgmental and emphasizes moving forward rather than simply looking back. In this way, the mutual assessment process can re-motivate everyone.

Making Changes
As with any program evaluation, it is only worth the effort if you are willing to analyze the results of the assessment and develop plans to implement necessary changes. If done correctly, an evaluation will point out areas of strength as well as of weakness, since improvement might come simply from doing more of what has been done right in the past. From the volunteer management perspective, the importance of evaluation is the need to be sure that volunteers are assigned to work that genuinely requires attention. Otherwise, volunteer effort is wasted on activities that are not useful. There is too much to be done to permit that.

THE DOLLAR VALUE
OF VOLUNTEERS

Evaluating volunteer program effectiveness provides you with information helpful in your administrative responsibilities. But so far we have only discussed the evaluation of volunteer activities, not the assessment of the financial value of volunteer involvement. This chapter presents a method available to you as executive for becoming more aware of the real cost of operating your organization.

Some of the information in this chapter has changed greatly in the ten years since the first edition of this book.[1] Recently, the accounting profession, the government, and even the public have become more involved in issues related to presenting the financial situation of nonprofit organizations. While most of the attention is focused on other accounting questions, for the first time volunteers are being seen as a resource with economic value. The rules have changed and ideas that we presented here ten years ago as innovative and even challenging to the accounting profession are now becoming "generally accepted accounting principles." There has been progress but with continuing controversy over whether and how best to measure the value of volunteer services.

Almost all nonprofit organizations receive in-kind contributions and the donation of services of a board of directors and other volunteers. Office space, printing, postage and a variety of other in-kind services are also often donated. All of these are of great importance to program services and all have a dollar value. Unfortunately, most nonprofits ignore such contributions on their financial statements—both those for internal use and those for external dissemination. In order for you to know how much it *really* costs to run your organization, a dollar value should be placed on volunteer time and in-kind contributions. These are as valuable as cash contributions.

Generally, volunteers have simply not been mentioned on nonprofit agency financial reports. This omission tends to *de*-value their services. To report that it cost $7,200 to winterize ten homebound elderly peoples' homes without mentioning the $4,000 *worth* of volunteer services or the $2,000 *worth* of donated supplies risks the reader forming some false conclusions about the actual cost of the service. From a management perspective, never having to "account" for the utilization of volunteers can result in wasting volunteer effort or in discounting its cost to the volunteer and its value to the organization.

The premise of this chapter can be summed up in the following formula:

Cash expenses plus the *value of contributed time and materials* equals the *true cost of service.*

Whether or not you wish to adopt all the steps of the method presented here, you may well want to consider how you can be certain that you (and your board or other decision-makers) base your planning on the most accurate picture of your resource expenditures. Further, managers tend to manage what is measured. So making an effort to reflect the dollar value of volunteers validates the importance of putting time and effort into working with them.

Why Compute Our True Costs?

You may be thinking, "I'm not sure we want to know the full cost of our program...We certainly don't want anyone else to compare how much our program really costs versus another program." Maybe you don't—but you as the administrator, and your board of directors, should be aware of the full costs of operating.

Clearly there are some philosophic issues at stake here. For example, some might argue that almost all nonprofits utilize volunteers as an inherent part of their operations. Such donated services are therefore "assumed" and there is no need to keep track of their dollar value. Furthermore, if people are willing to volunteer their time to an organization, should the value of that time be measured? Or is the volunteering itself "proof of the value" of the program? The argument includes the belief that it is hard to keep records anyway and the costs of doing so cannot be justified by the benefits of keeping track of volunteers' value.

Another issue relates to the "bottom line." Profit-making organizations have the "bottom line" of whether or not they make a profit. Sales measure whether the public thinks the company is making a desirable product or providing a worthwhile service. Should nonprofits be treated differently? If a social good is being provided, should cost be considered?

We could also ask whether one nonprofit should be compared to another on the basis of how much money each spends to provide its services. Should an alcohol rehabilitation program be compared to another alcohol rehabilitation program on any basis other than the effectiveness of their programs?

An additional problem inherent in keeping track of volunteer services is that valuing donated time and materials and including them in your financial statements will increase the apparent size of the organization. Will this be seen as an attempt to inflate the figures to make the agency look bigger than it is? Might it affect how some grant makers compute your overhead allowance? Will it make the agency appear "rich"? Will such conclusions make potential donors think you do not need their money?

None of these questions has an easy answer, but there are strong arguments in favor of keeping track of your donated time and materials.

Your board of directors and funding sources, both current and potential, are interested in what your resources are and how you use them—and donated time and materials are a very significant resource. Properly presented, inclusion of donated time and materials in your financial statements may impress potential funders with the degree of support demonstrated by the community—and with your managerial sophistication at recognizing the value of such support. Funding sources may see the value of volunteer service as "leverage" for their money. The funder's dollar contribution to your program has the potential to generate two, five or twenty times its worth through the value of volunteer time and in-kind materials. But you can best make this point by keeping records of donated time and materials and putting a dollar value on them.

Certain donors and government grant-making agencies will accept volunteer time as in-kind "matching funds" on grant applications. Again, you will need to be able to document any value you place on such contributed services.

There are internal management reasons for wanting to keep records on volunteers, too. You need to be able to recognize and thank volunteers. It is much more meaningful to thank someone for 105 hours, or for five hours a week for ten weeks, than for "all your time." (Even more important is acknowledging specific results and end products of the contributed time.)

It is therefore essential to keep records of volunteer time and determine a dollar value for that time, at least for internal purposes. You may, initially, decide you do not need to record the value in your accounting records. At a minimum, making a start at valuing the contributions of volunteers should give you and your board a more significant and valid picture of the cost of human effort you expend in delivering services. As presented in Chapter 3, your organization is incurring costs to facilitate the work of volunteers, both to purchase tangible equipment and supplies and in paid staff time. Calculating the dollar value of volunteer services therefore shows the revenue/support gained by these expenses.

Keeping Track of Donated Time

How do you keep track of donated time? The method is very similar to how you keep track of time for which you pay: by using time records of various kinds.[2] It is also important, for accounting purposes, to have all staff members (paid and unpaid) allocate their recorded time, at least by: 1) each major program or service category; 2) management and general administration; 3) membership development; and 4) fundraising. This information may be needed to prepare your financial statements and the report to the Federal government (Form 990), both of which require that expenses be broken out into these categories (at a minimum).

Once you have recorded accumulated volunteer hours, you can calculate their value by multiplying hours by an appropriate hourly rate for each of the jobs performed.

One of the objections often raised about keeping track of volunteer hours is that it is difficult, if not impossible, to get volunteers in all categories to keep a record of the time they contribute. This may be true, but the solution is to aim for recording as much of the time as possible, not to ignore recording some because you cannot record all. You can begin to apply the following valuation system to whatever number of hours you have gathered for volunteer service.

Most administrators are justifiably concerned with measuring the "cost effectiveness" of agency projects—whether the funds and staff

Dollar Value of Volunteers

time expended are commensurate with the value of the service provided. Cost effectiveness is easy to prove for a volunteer program. The actual cost of salarying the program staff, paying for supplies, and other expenses is "leverage" money that produces many multiples of hours of volunteer service than that same amount of money could have "paid" for hours of employee time. (However, this argument is only valid if the evaluation of the quality of volunteer service concludes that something meaningful was produced!)

In order to generate the most useful data, take the time to estimate the dollar value of volunteers as fairly as possible. Do *not* fall into the common trap of using the minimum wage or the national median wage as a basis for your computation. The vast majority of volunteer assignments are worth a great deal more than minimum wage and probably more than the median, too.

One other trap is to confuse the dollar value of the service provided by volunteers with the earning power of the people who are doing the volunteering. If someone earns his or her living as a lawyer, teacher, or doctor and volunteers to write a brief, teach classes, or do blood tests for your organization—then you are justified to estimate the dollar value of those donated services at the hourly rate normally charged by that volunteer. But if that same lawyer, teacher or doctor volunteers to paint your rec hall, drive clients to a picnic, or play chess with residents—the dollar value of his or her volunteer work has nothing to do with his or her regular earning power. You must assess the value of each volunteer assignment based on what it would cost you to purchase that type of work in the marketplace.

The best system for determining the true dollar value of volunteer services was developed by G. Neil Karn while he served as director of the Virginia Department of Volunteerism.[3]

He details his approach at great length, but here are his key points:

1. It is possible to find an equivalent salaried job category for every volunteer assignment, even if it means a little creativity and searching. Each volunteer assignment should be given its own dollar equivalency, without trying to find an average rate for all volunteers.

2. The cost of paying an employee includes fringe benefits that raise the total value of the "annual employee compensation package" considerably.

3. We routinely pay salaried staff for hours they do not work, while we credit volunteers only for hours they actually put in.

4. Volunteers should be "credited" with the dollar equivalent of the hourly amount an employee would earn for actual hours worked.

The illustration to the right shows the way to compute the value of volunteer services using the Karn method.

By using the volunteer job description for each assignment, it is possible to compare the tasks given to volunteers to those listed in the job descriptions for employees *somewhere*. This may require some research to identify paid job classifications. The local offices of the United States' and your state's Department of Labor maintain useful listings of job categories and pay scales in your geographic region. Some of the actual equivalent job categories in Virginia that Karn uses as examples are:

VOLUNTEER ASSIGNMENT	EQUIVALENT PAID CLASSIFICATION
Criminal justice one-to-one visitor	Probation and parole officer trainee
Volunteer member of a conference planning committee	Human resource developer
Little League coach	Playground supervisor
Little League official	Recreation specialist
Big Brother/Sister	Outreach worker
Board member	Executive Director

TRUE DOLLAR VALUE OF VOLUNTEERS
WORKSHEET

Volunteer Job Title: _____

    I. Equivalent Salaried Job Classification
       (Based on a comparison of the tasks and responsibilities
       described in the volunteer job description with those of an
       equivalent employee.)

       Equivalent Salaried Job Title: _____

    II. Annual Salary for Equivalent Salaried Classification: $_____

   III. Value of Benefits Package:
          FICA $_____
          Health Insurance   _____
          Life Insurance   _____
          Workers Compensation Insurance _____
          Retirement   _____
          Other Benefits: _____ _____
                    Total Value of Benefits: $_____

   IV. Annual Salary **+** Benefits Package =
       TOTAL ANNUAL COMPENSATION PACKAGE: $_____

    V. Established Annual Work Hours for
       Agency:_____hours/week X 52 weeks =   _____ hours

   VI. Hours Paid but Not Worked Annually:
          Annual Leave   _____ hours
          Paid Holidays   _____
          Paid Sick Leave   _____
                 Total Hours Paid/Not Worked: _____

  VII. Established Annual Hours - Hours
      Paid but Not Worked =
      ACTUAL WORK HOURS ANNUALLY: _____ hours

 VIII. **TOTAL ANNUAL COMPENSATION PACKAGE ÷**
      ACTUAL WORK HOURS ANNUALLY =

      TRUE DOLLAR VALUE OF EACH
      HOUR OF VOLUNTEER TIME IN
      THIS JOB DESCRIPTION: $_____

For some volunteer jobs, the equivalent paid classification will be more obvious. For example, a volunteer assigned to help with mass mailings and photocopying would be equivalent to an entry-level clerk or secretary position. A volunteer writing your newsletter would be equivalent to a public relations specialist or editor.

Also, the qualifications of each volunteer may be an important factor in measuring the cost of volunteer service. If someone comes to you with experience in the type of assignment s/he will carry, that volunteer's dollar equivalent is higher than a "trainee" level. Similarly, if a volunteer has been with your organization for several years, that person's equivalent wage would be higher than a new volunteer's/employee's.

Once you have identified the equivalent paid classification and its annual salary, you next must add the value of a typical *benefits* package: FICA, retirement, insurances, and other benefits. The total dollar amount of the benefits package and the salary equals the "Annual Compensation Package" for an employee in that position.

Now compute how many *hours* a year your organization has established as expected work hours. For example, 40 hours per week times 52 weeks per year equals 2080 hours per year. Using this as a base, add up the hours for which employees are paid but do not work. This includes annual leave (vacation), paid holidays, paid sick leave, and paid personal leave. For many organizations, this can total over 200 hours per year. Now subtract this from the total number of work hours per year to arrive at "Actual Work Hours Annually."

By dividing the Actual Work Hours Annually into the Annual Compensation Package, you arrive at the *"True Hourly Value."* It is *this* hourly rate that should be used in determining the dollar value of volunteer service. And as Karn says, this figure should be presented unapologetically!

A number of administrators have questioned this high dollar value because volunteers are rarely, if ever, full-time workers and so would not qualify for a benefits package. Karn answers this objection by pointing out three economic realities in the paid workforce. First, organizations commonly pay hourly or part-time workers at a higher hourly rate than full-time workers because part-timers do not receive benefits. Similarly, help hired through a   temporary employment agency also costs more per hour, to cover both the agency's profit margin and some benefits the agency may pay to its employees. So if you prefer using the model of the temporary employee to be the measure of volunteer economic worth, you would still wind up with a dollar value higher than the equivalent of the base salary of a full-time employee for each hour served. Finally, organizations pay premium prices for the time of a consultant with technical expertise, which is another way of looking at many volunteer services.[4]

The good news is that the best computer software programs designed to manage volunteer program data allow you to enter a dollar value for each job description and then automatically calculate totals for each assignment and for all volunteers. You must do the work upfront to determine the dollar value, but then you can let technology take over!

Other Dollar Value Options

The Karn method of valuing volunteer time remains the most highly regarded. But because it is time-consuming to implement initially, some agencies have developed simpler ways of calculating a dollar value. For example, it is possible to take the total annual agency budget for wages and benefits and divide it by the number of hours worked by employees on the payroll. This provides an average hourly wage *for your agency* which can be used to estimate the value of volunteer time. This method acknowledges that volunteers do a variety of tasks, comparable to various levels of paid staff, and also adds in the amount spent on benefits.

Your state's Department of Labor may keep regional statistics on average salaries for the general categories of staff in your agency. This allows you to use labor costs in your own area, rather than a national aggregate. Always remember to add in benefits packages, for which the Department of Labor can also supply average percentages.

Whatever method you use, do everything possible to avoid relying on the minimum wage as the standard value of volunteer time.

Your Financial Records

Just as you should involve your accountant or finance officer in financial considerations, I, too, have consulted a CPA to participate in writing the following discussion of accounting practices. He is Alan S.Glazer, Professor of Business Administration at Franklin & Marshall College in Lancaster, Pennsylvania. Alan has been deeply involved in the development of the new regulations for nonprofit accounting and was a consultant to the Not-for-Profit Organizations Committee of the American Institute of Certified Public Accountants. He has also co-authored a number of articles explaining the new regulations, including "Implementing FASB 116 and 117" in the Journal of Accountancy, September *1995. He gets to practice what he preaches by serving on several nonprofit boards.*

Let's turn to how to record the dollar equivalency amount of volunteer service in your agency's internal and external financial reports.

Your Internal Financial Reports

You, other members of management, and your board need to have financial information for budget and decision-making purposes that reflects the total dollar cost of all the people who work on behalf of your agency. The total cost of your paid staff comes directly from your payroll records, and the dollar value of volunteer services can be estimated using the Karn method just described or a simpler one. Your internal financial reports should show the dollar value of volunteer services as both expense and contribution revenue. True, it has no impact on your "bottom line," but it does enable you to show a more complete picture of your organization's programs and supporting activities.

As already advised in Chapter 1, no matter what, never use the phrase "volunteers *save* us money." This statement implies that you had resources you did not need to spend because volunteers are free. A better and more accurate way to make the same point would be: "volunteers *extend our budget* beyond anything we would otherwise be able to afford."

Since the publication of this book's first edition, the accounting profession has given serious consideration to nonprofit's external financial statements.

Your External Financial Statements

The Financial Accounting Standards Board (FASB), the profession's most important rule-making group, recognizes that "differences between nonbusiness organizations and business enterprises arise principally in the way they obtain resources."[5] As a result of those differences, FASB has issued several new rules that pertain to nonprofits. The American Institute of Certified Public Accountants (AICPA) has developed two new industry guides to help accountants and auditors implement the requirements.[6]

One of the most important new rules, FASB Statement No. 116,[7] requires nonprofits to report certain contributions received from donors, including volunteer services. Here are the parts that deal with contributed services:

> 9. *Contributions of services shall be recognized [at fair value] if the services received (a) create or enhance nonfinancial assets or (b) require specialized skills, are provided by individuals possessing those skills, and would typically need to be purchased if not provided by donation. Services requiring specialized skills are provided by accountants, architects, carpenters, doctors, electricians, lawyers, nurses, plumbers, teachers, and other professionals and craftsmen. Contributed services and promises to give services that do not meet the above criteria shall not be recognized.*
>
> . . . .
>
> 19. *Quoted market prices, if available, are the best evidence of the fair value of monetary and nonmonetary assets, including services. If quoted market prices are not available, fair value may be estimated based on quoted market prices for similar assets, independent appraisals, or valuation techniques, such as the present value of estimated future cash flows. Contributions of services that create or enhance nonfinancial assets may be measured by referring to either the fair value of the services received or the fair value of the asset or of the asset enhancement resulting from the services. A major uncertainty about the existence of value may indicate that an item received or given should not be recognized.*[8]

These rules mean that, for the first time. your agency may need to include the value of certain volunteer services in its external financial statements. The services that meet the criteria described above must be recorded as revenues or gains in the year in which your agency receives the services. At the same time, the services are recorded either as expenses (if they provide no future benefit) or as part of long-term assets (if they create or enhance assets such as buildings, inventory, and equipment).

Under the FASB rules, not all volunteer services must be recorded. For example, a volunteer whom you train to be a guide, does not necessarily have "specialized skills." However, the time of a lawyer who contributes free legal service or a carpenter who builds new storage space may have to be included in your financial statements.

Let's consider three other examples of how these new rules apply:

—Nonprofit A begins to construct a new facility to house its programs. It incurs a total cost of $75,000 to acquire land and to obtain necessary permits. A local contractor volunteers to contribute the materials and to build the facility for Nonprofit A. Upon completion, the facility (including the land) is estimated to have an appraised value of $125,000. Nonprofit A must record contributed services revenue of $50,000 because the contractor's services create a nonfinancial asset, the new facility, with a value of $50,000. The facility should be recorded as an asset of $50,000.

—Nonprofit B employs both paid and unpaid teachers. The unpaid teachers volunteer their services because they are members of a religious order. Both types of teachers have similar duties, responsibilities, and teaching qualifications. Nonprofit B should include both contributed services revenue and salaries expense for the services contributed by the unpaid teachers. Teaching requires special skills; the unpaid teachers have those skills, which would have been purchased by Nonprofit B had the unpaid teachers not contributed their time. To estimate the value of the unpaid teachers' time, Nonprofit B could use either the Karn method or the salaries of paid teachers with similar qualifications, experience, and duties.

—One of the members of Nonprofit C's board of trustees is an accountant who has served for many years. The accountant has occasionally provided routine business advice to management and the board, but refers all substantive questions to the organization's CPA firm. Nonprofit C should not include the fair value of the board member's services in its financial statements. Those services do not require specialized skills because the board member did not answer any complex questions requiring an accountant's specialized skills.

Even if contributed services are not recorded in the external financial statements, the FASB requires that information about contributed services be included in the notes to those statements. This additional requirement is:

10. An entity that receives contributed services shall describe the programs or activities for which those services were used, including the nature and extent of contributed services received for the period and the amount recognized as revenues for the period. Entities are encouraged to disclose the fair value of contributed services received but not recognized as revenues if that is practicable.[9]

This means that you should include descriptive information in your external financial statements about the types of contributed services your agency receives. That information should help the readers of your statements understand the nature of your programs and supporting activities and the extent to which you depend on contributed services. Here are two examples of notes to financial statements that discuss volunteer services:

Example 1:

No amounts have been reflected in the financial statements for donated services. The UW pays for most services requiring specific expertise. However, many individuals volunteer their time and perform a variety of tasks that assist the UW with specific assistance programs, campaign solicitations, and various committee assignments. The UW receives more than 12,000 volunteer hours per year.[10]

Example 2:

The organization recognizes contribution revenue for certain services at the fair value of those services. Those services include the following items:

	19X1	19X0
Home outreach program:		
Salaries:		
Social work interns—261 and 315 hours at $12.00 per hour	$ 3,132	$ 3,780
Registered nurses—200 and 220 hours at $15.00 per hour	3,000	3,300
Total salaries	6,132	7,080
Management and general:		
Accounting services	10,000	19,000
Total contributed services	$16,132	$26,080

In addition, approximately 80,000 hours, for which no value has been assigned, were volunteered by tutors in the home outreach program.[11]

Both of these notes meet the FASB's minimum requirements. But which better conveys the importance of the agency's volunteers? As previously demonstrated, it is possible to measure, on an objective, verifiable basis, the value of contributed services. It requires the agency to keep records. This may be a difficult job, particularly at first, but it can be done.

You'll need an information system that:

—Distinguishes between contributed services that must be recorded in the financial statements under FASB rules and those that cannot be recorded.

—Captures information describing the programs and supporting activities for which volunteer services are used.

—Develops numerical information to be used to estimate the value of those services. (The Karn method described earlier is an example of such information.)

Too many nonprofits have not kept accurate records of volunteer time and have made only a minimal attempt to assign a dollar value to such time. In the past, CPAs accepted this without questioning the validity of the omission or suggesting possible approaches to documenting dollar values, because accounting rules did not require disclosure of contributed services. Because of the new FASB rules, this would be a perfect time to work with your CPA and use the methods suggested in this chapter to estimate the value of one of your organization's most valuable resources—volunteer time.

Other Contributions

As we've seen, communicating information about the total resources available to your organization requires including the value of contributed services. In addition, many nonprofits receive other forms of contributions, including cash, securities, inventory, supplies, land, buildings, the use of facilities and utilities, and pledges to contribute those items in the future. FASB and AICPA rules now require that the fair value of many of those contributions be included in nonprofits' external financial statements. These rules can be summarized as follows:

—Contributions should be reported as revenues (or gains) and as assets in the period received. This includes pledges (which FASB calls "promises to give") that are made unconditionally by donors.

—Contributions received must be classified as permanent-
ly restricted, temporarily restricted or unrestricted,
depending on the presence and type of donor-imposed
restrictions.

—Contributed assets that can be resold or used by the
organization are measured at their fair value based on
quoted market prices. If such prices are unavailable,
other estimates of fair value, such as the prices of similar assets or average values per pound, can be used.

—If the items received have no value (for example, used
clothing that cannot be used for program purposes or
resold in a thrift shop), they should not be included in
the financial statements.

—Contributions of the use of utilities, facilities, and other
long-term assets must be reported as revenues when
received and as expenses in the periods in which the
utilities and assets are used.

—Contributions of art, historical treasures, and similar
items (called "collection items" by FASB) may not have
to be reported in financial statements under certain circumstances.

Implementing these new rules is complex and should be
discussed with your financial officer and CPA if your agency
receives a significant amount of contributions. The important
word here is "significant." If your organization receives donated
assets or facilities and they are significant to your program,
include them in your internal financial reports and external financial statements. As you might guess, the definition of "significant"
is not easy. Here is a suggested guideline: if, in describing your
program, leaving out a specific element would be a distortion,
confuse your explanation or be misleading, then that specific element is "significant."

Many nonprofit organizations tell business people about
the tax advantages of contributing inventory or items held for
ordinary sale to a charitable organization. Technically this is correct. A corporation may deduct its basis (tax accounting jargon for

"cost") for the contributed property plus one-half of the property's appreciated value (that is, market value), but the deduction cannot exceed twice the property's basis (cost). The actual wording of the tax code is really much more complicated, but this is a paraphrase. For most donations, a business will deduct its inventory cost, the same value as if it threw the item away.

An additional rationale for making the effort to document and value donated materials is for budget preparation. If, for example, this year your organization receives $1,400 in donated light bulbs and you do not record this, at the time you prepare next year's budget, you may be inclined to include nothing in the maintenance line item for light bulbs. If this turns out to be a one-time contribution, you have under-budgeted an expense that will have to be covered and have overlooked a dollar amount that must be included in your fundraising efforts.

Sample Statement of Activities

On the next page is an example of the form in which contributed services and contributions of other resources might appear in an agency's statement of activities under the new FASB regulations.[12]

The Internal Revenue Service

The IRS is ambivalent about what information it wants from nonprofit organizations. On the one hand, Form 990, Part VII ("Other Information"), asks the question: "Did your organization receive donated services or the use of materials, equipment or facilities at no charge or at substantially less than fair rental value?" If you answer "yes," there is a line on which you may indicate the value of such items. This means that the IRS recognizes the prevalence and importance of this type of donation to nonprofits, though it makes the reporting of such data optional.

On the other hand, there are clear instructions that the amount reported for donated services and materials may not be included elsewhere on the Form 990 as part of the organization's "support" or "expense." This perpetuates the concept that only transactions involving cash should be used in measuring the financial results of a nonprofit organization.

Newtown Agency
Statement of Activities
Year Ended June 30, 19X6

	Unrestricted	Temporarily Restricted	Permanently Restricted	Total
Revenues, gains, and other support:				
Contributions: (See note A)				
Cash	$ XXX	XX	XX	XXX
In-kind	X			X
Promises to give	XX	XX	XX	XXX
Volunteer services	XX			XX
Total contributions	XXXX	XXX	XXX	XXXXX
Fees	XXX			XXX
Other income	X			X
Total	XXXXX	XXX	XXX	XXXXX
Expenses and losses:				
Program A	XXXX			XXXX
Program B	XXXX			XXXX
Management & general	XX			XX
Fundraising	XX			XX
Other expenses and losses	X			X
Total	XXXXX			XXXXX
Changes in net assets	XX	XXX	XXX	XXX
Net assets at beginning of year	XXX	XXX	XXX	XXXX
Net assets at end of year	XXX	XXX	XXX	XXXX

Volunteers should be informed that **Tax Issues**
they can take certain deductions
on their Federal income tax returns
for some of the expenses incurred
in their volunteer work. These contributions are all included as
cash contributions on Schedule A of the volunteer's personal
income tax return (Form 1040).

Basically, this means certain unreimbursed, out-of-pocket
costs such as auto mileage (at 12 cents per mile in 1996, as it was
in 1986); parking; tolls; train, bus or cab fares; travel expenses,
lodging and meals for overnight trips; uniforms; telephone bills;
office supplies; etc. Also, expenses spent *on* the service-user are
deductible. For example, a Big Sister who takes her Little Sister to
the zoo may deduct the admission price for her Little Sister—but
not for herself.

Other items that are not deductible include the value of
time donated (at any hourly rate), child care expenses, and meals
(unless the volunteer is away overnight).

Your organization may, of course, reimburse volunteers for
any expenses they incur on your behalf. Such reimbursement is
not considered "income" to them for tax purposes. Be aware,
however, that if you give volunteers a predetermined "allowance"
for expenses without documentation of actual costs incurred, any
excess over actual reimbursement may indeed become taxable
income to the volunteer.

It makes sense that if volunteers spend money for you and
are not reimbursed, they have made a "contribution" to your
organization. If you ask your volunteers to keep track of the items
on which they spend money and give you a copy of their listing,
there are benefits to both of you. You help them to keep records
of possible Federal income tax deductions they might otherwise
overlook. And you have documentation for recording these
amounts as contributions to your organization.

Some organizations offer volunteers a stipend as a form of
enabling funds. If you do this, consult your accountant about the
dollar amount and the potential tax implications of this practice.
It is important to protect your organization from charges of wage
and Social Security tax avoidance and to assure that you do not
create taxable income for individual volunteers.

The Value of   As mentioned briefly above, the
Personal Services   value of personal service given to
                                a charitable organization is not
                                deductible by an individual volun-
teer as a contribution. This is true whether the volunteer is self-
employed or works for a company. In many cases, companies
allow employees to do charitable work on company time, while
on salary. This would usually be deductible *by the company* as an
operating salary expense, but not as a contribution, unless the
amount becomes significant enough to warrant other treatment.

Sometimes an individual will suggest giving your organization an invoice for hours worked and then donating the fee back
to the agency. This sounds fine, but upon closer examination has
no benefit to either party and, in fact, can cause a tax liability to
the individual volunteer. The volunteer in this transaction would
need to record the invoice as "income" but would also have the
contribution "expense"—and the net result would be zero. But
some taxes are based on gross receipts (billings), so the volunteer would be taxed on the value of the invoice, even if later
donating the money back. Also, a corporation might have a loss
and therefore not be able to deduct the contribution in the year
it was made. In neither case is much gained.

However, some volunteers (those who are contributing
their professional services) may want to prepare an invoice, giving a dollar amount for the services rendered, but marked with
some appropriate wording such as "cancelled—contributed time."
This invoice, needing no payment from your agency, provides a
basis for the amount to be recorded as donated services in your
financial reports. Legally, the volunteers do not have to record the
cancelled invoice on their financial records, but the invoice gives
them some documentation of their time.

Sometimes individuals or organizations provide services (or
goods) to nonprofits at a discount price. At the time of invoic-
ing, you should request that the bill show the full fair market
value of the services (or goods), as well as the discount. In this
way you establish a more accurate base for future budgeting and
fundraising. Of course, the discount may have to be recorded on
your financial statements as a contribution.

As executive director, you must **It's Up to You**
have a complete understanding of
the financial aspects of your
agency. The procedures described
in this chapter will help you achieve this goal. Only with a total
picture of your organization's resources and how they are used
can you adequately explain them to your board and potential
funders. This knowledge is also needed to manage your organization on a day-to-day basis.

[1]Acknowledgment is given to the CPA who contributed to the original
version of this chapter in the first edition, John Paul Dalsimer.

[2]Susan J. Ellis and Katherine H. Noyes, *Proof Positive: Developing
Significant Recordkeeping Systems*, revised ed., Philadelphia: Energize, 1990.

[3]G. Neil Karn, "The True Dollar Value of Volunteers," *The Journal of
Volunteer Administration*, Vol. I, No. 2 (Winter 1982-83), pp. 1-17 and Vol. I, No.
3 (Spring 1983), pp. 1-19.

[4]G. Neil Karn, "Addendum to 'Money Talks," *The Journal of Volunteer
Administration*, Vol. III, No. 1 (Fall 1984), pp. 12-13.

[5]FASB, *Statement of Financial Accounting Concepts No. 4, Objectives of
Financial Reporting by Nonbusiness Organizations*, 1980, para.15.

[6]*Not-for-Profit Organizations* (in press) and *Audits of Health-Care
Organizations* (in press).

[7]FASB, *Statement of Financial Accounting Standards No. 116,
Accounting for Contributions Received and Contributions Made*, 1993.

[8]*Ibid.*, para. 9 and 19 (footnote omitted).

[9]*Ibid.*, para. 10.

[10]FASB, *Results of the Field Test of the Proposed Standards for Financial
Statements of Not-for-Profit Organizations and Accounting for Contributions*,
1994, p. 85.

[11]AICPA, Exposure Draft: *Audit and Accounting Guide, Not-for-Profit
Organizations*, 1995, para. 5.59.

[12]FASB, *Statement of Financial Accounting Standards No. 117,
Financial Statements of Not-for-Profit Organizations*, 1993.

EXECUTIVE ROLE CHECKLIST

On a daily basis, the top executive has an important role in demonstrating institutional and personal support for the volunteer program within the organization s/he runs. The following is a summary of the basic elements of a successful volunteer program. Each element is described briefly, followed by a very specific set of responsibilities that belong to you—as the top executive—regardless of whom you have actually designated as head of the volunteer program. These are actions that require your leadership and authority. Some have been mentioned already throughout the book but are summarized here as well to give you the complete picture.

You can use this as a checklist to assess your present level of participation in your organization's volunteer program...and to set goals for your future involvement in assuring the success of volunteers.

1. Planning and Resource Allocation

Planning is the key to success in all administrative responsibilities and volunteer management is no exception. Planning for volunteers involves the need to determine: exactly why volunteers are wanted; exactly what volunteers are expected to do; what resources will be necessary to support the work of volunteers; who will be designated to lead the volunteer effort; who will provide training and ongoing supervision of volunteers; and what preparation these key people will need.

EXECUTIVE ROLE:

☐ Develop the goals and objectives, and then the policies and procedures, for volunteer involvement. Write and disseminate a "Statement of Philosophy" regarding volunteers.

☐ Place the subject of volunteers and community involvement on the agenda of board meetings at least annually.

☐ Staff the volunteer program appropriately.

☐ Assure that the volunteer program leader answers to the most logical administrator.

☐ Make yourself accessible if and when special questions needing decision-making authority arise concerning the involvement of volunteers.

☐ Budget funds and allocate other resources appropriately. Recognize the dollar value of volunteers as an important contribution to your organization.

☐ Make sure that all employees are trained to work effectively with volunteers and participate in identifying categories of work for volunteers.

☐ Assure that good risk management practices are implemented to keep volunteers, staff and recipients of services as safe as possible.

☐ Include the director of volunteers in future planning for the organization.

☐ Allow volunteers to experiment for you by testing new ideas that may later be fundable.

2. Volunteer Job Descriptions

If an assignment cannot be described in writing, it probably is not a job. To assure effective utilization of volunteers, define the work to be done as specifically as possible. Volunteer job descriptions should, at a minimum, define: a title for the position; the purpose/rationale for the position; the scope of the work to be done (giving both the potential and limits of the job); the plan for training and supervision/collaboration; and the necessary timeframes. It is also important to determine how many hours of work will be needed to fulfill the function—not how many people (since volunteers have varied work schedules).

EXECUTIVE ROLE:

☐ Insist on having volunteer job descriptions put in writing.

☐ Make sure every unit and every administrative level in the organization submits requests for volunteers.

☐ Uphold the authority of the director of volunteers to say "no" to an inappropriate request for volunteers.

☐ Develop job descriptions for volunteers to assist you directly, to model your personal acceptance of volunteer talents.

3. Recruitment/Public Relations

"Public relations" is what makes an organization visible to the public. It is necessary to have visibility and a good image so that people might consider volunteering for you. "Recruitment" is the process of encouraging people to give their time and energy to your organization. The best recruitment is targeted to the audiences most likely to have the skills and interests to match the available volunteer job descriptions.

EXECUTIVE ROLE:

☐ Be sure that the volunteer program (and therefore the opportunity to apply to become a volunteer) is mentioned in agency descriptive materials, annual reports and other public relations vehicles.

☐ Keep the director of volunteers informed of your speaking schedule and distribute volunteer recruitment materials whenever you distribute other agency literature.

☐ Invite the director of volunteers to accompany you to community events at which recruitment might be possible.

4. Screening and Selection

Many supervision and management problems can be prevented by effective initial interviewing of prospective volunteers. The screening (including screening out, if necessary) and selection process surfaces the expectations of the applicant and allows the director of volunteers to explain the standards of the organization. Also, each new volunteer should be matched to the most appropriate assignment.

EXECUTIVE ROLE:

☐ Back up the director of volunteer's right to screen out inappropriate candidates.

☐ Expect the director of volunteers to question people who apply to volunteer even if they are related to or referred by other salaried staff, board members, funders, or other influential people.

☐ Tell the personnel department not to send rejected job applicants to the volunteer office with the suggestion that volunteering is an alternative to employment with you (unless they are really appropriate candidates to be good volunteers).

☐ Apply the same hiring procedures and standards to volunteers as to employees, particularly avoiding discrimination.

5. Orientation

Orientation is the overview of the total organization necessary for every new volunteer, regardless of specific assignment. It places the work into context and allows for consistent introduction of policies, procedures, rights, and responsibilities.

EXECUTIVE ROLE:

☐ Participate in the welcoming of new volunteers (either in person each time, through videotape, or by a letter of greeting).

☐ Review the content of the orientation to be sure it represents the agency as you wish it to.

6. Volunteer Training

Training is individualized and should vary with the demands of each specific volunteer job description and the background each volunteer brings to the organization. There is the need for initial, start-up training, plus the need for ongoing, in-service training. Much "training" is really the giving of good instructions and is often integrated into the overall supervision plan.

EXECUTIVE ROLE:

☐ Assure that all volunteers receive training appropriate to their needs and job descriptions.

☐ Recognize that it will take staff time to train volunteers and adjust workload demands accordingly.

☐ Develop a training plan for volunteers assigned directly to you.

7. Supervision of Volunteers

As with salaried staff, volunteer staff need support from those in a position to see the total picture and who know what work needs to be done. For volunteers, however, a key aspect of supervision is access to someone in charge during the actual time the volunteer is on duty or when the volunteer who is working independently in the field needs a question answered.

EXECUTIVE ROLE:

☐ Again, recognize that it will take staff time to supervise volunteers well.

☐ Clarify that volunteers are the responsibility of all staff members—and that volunteers do not "belong" to the director of volunteers.

☐ Include volunteers on the organizational chart under each unit in which they are active.

☐ Reserve time to supervise volunteers assigned directly to you.

☐ Clarify lines of responsibility between the organization and any independently-organized volunteer advocacy support/ fundraising group such as an auxiliary. Be accessible to the officers of such groups and make sure they are kept informed about agency plans.

8. Recognition

Recognition is one way we "pay" volunteers for their efforts, but it has many nuances. If there is an annual banquet, but no daily support, recognition is given "with forked tongue"! While formalized, annual thank-you events are worthwhile, informal, continuous recognition is more important. This includes everything from simple courtesy to including volunteers in staff meetings and decision-making. It is also a part of recognition to offer constructive criticism, since such training implies a belief that the volunteer can do even better work.

EXECUTIVE ROLE:

☐ Be visible to volunteers year round and take time to interact with them occasionally in an informal manner.

☐ Participate in formal recognition events, whether as a speaker, in signing certificates, or by simply taking part. Write your own speeches and show how informed you are about the work volunteers are doing. Stay for the whole event.

☐ Encourage board members to attend volunteer recognition events, both because they, too, deserve thanks for their contributed efforts and to show that they value the volunteer services of others.

☐ Periodically share updates on new agency developments, future plans, etc.—especially those that will affect volunteers.

☐ Provide visible recognition to employees who have been successful in working with volunteers.

9. Coordination

Almost always, volunteers are part-time staff. A volunteer program can have people who work once a year or regularly on schedules ranging from one afternoon a week to four days a week; mornings and evenings; alternate Sundays; etc. Add to this the diversity of the people who volunteer (all ages, backgrounds, physical conditions, academic degrees), and you end up with an amazing logistical challenge. A volunteer program must have a leader— and leadership includes coordinating all the details of scheduling and assigning.

EXECUTIVE ROLE:

☐ Assure that any and all people who help your organization without going on the payroll are registered with the volunteer office, regardless of who recruits or supervises them: student interns, holiday helpers, expert advisors contributing their time on a *pro bono* basis.

☐ Recognize the unique nature of the volunteer scheduling pattern (diverse part-time hours) and make sure agency services can respond. For example, assure that everyone recognizes the importance of taking messages when the director of volunteers is unavailable, or keep evening reception desk staff informed about volunteer projects underway in the evenings.

☐ Assign adequate staff leadership to the volunteer program. At a minimum, designate evening, night or weekend supervisors responsible in the absence of the director of volunteers.

☐ Require that other departments coordinate public outreach activities cooperatively with the director of volunteers, particularly public relations, development, and special events.

10. Recordkeeping and Reporting

If volunteers are important to the work of the organization, then it is important to know what volunteers are doing. Such documentation assists in recruitment, training, recognition, and fundraising. For purposes of insurance and to back up the income tax deduction claims of volunteers, recordkeeping by the agency is also vital. Once records are kept, they are of little meaning if they are not reported. Reports of the cumulative achievements of volunteers should be shared routinely with the volunteers themselves, as well as with top administration and funding sources.

EXECUTIVE ROLE:

☐ Expect to receive useful reports from the director of volunteers.

☐ Read and react to reports when submitted.

☐ Purchase computer software designed for the special needs of volunteer management and/or insist that the agency's computer programmers work with the director of volunteers to make the computer program do what is necessary to manage volunteers better.

☐ Make sure each department submits forms and other necessary data about volunteers to the volunteer office in a timely and complete fashion.

☐ Look for (and ask for) mention of volunteer activities in the reports of other department heads or staff members.

☐ Include data on the volunteer program in reports you make to the board or to funders. Also include such data in agency annual reports.

11. Evaluation

It is sinful to waste the time of a volunteer. Therefore it is imperative that volunteer programs regularly evaluate the impact of services performed and whether those services are still necessary. Along with program evaluation, it is helpful to conduct individual performance reviews with volunteers, so as to maintain motivation, troubleshoot potential problem areas, and allow for personal growth.

EXECUTIVE ROLE:

☐ Insist on performance—hold volunteers accountable to meeting goals and being productive.

☐ Include assessment of the volunteer program in any agency evaluation.

☐ Evaluate the director of volunteers on his/her ability to develop a volunteer program that taps a wide variety of community resources and responds to current trends in volunteerism.

☐ Evaluate salaried staff on the criterion of how well they have worked with volunteers during the period being assessed.

☐ Ask volunteers for their perspective, opinions, and suggestions on the operational effectiveness of the organization.

12. Volunteer/Employee Relations

The interrelationship of volunteers and salaried staff is the single biggest pitfall to volunteer program success, unless steps are taken early to encourage teamwork. There are numerous reasons why salaried staff are threatened by volunteers or why volunteers may be resistant to working well with employees. This is a human relations issue with no easy answers, but it should be remembered that almost no professional/academic training program prepares salaried staff to work with volunteers. So staff development training on this topic is vital. Clarification of roles and commitment from top administration are critical aspects to success in this area.

EXECUTIVE ROLE:

☐ Provide training for employees on the subject of working with volunteers successfully.

☐ Monitor the degree of acceptance of volunteers by the salaried staff. Provide positive and negative sanctions for working or not working well with volunteers.

☐ Include questions about past experience working with volunteers and being a volunteer on agency employment application forms/interviews.

☐ Include "supervision of volunteers" in the job description of any staff member who will be working with volunteers.

☐ Approach specific interpersonal problems between members of staff and particular volunteers objectively. Do not tip the scales in favor of the employee before hearing all the facts and be open to deciding that the volunteer may be right.

☐ Negotiate with union leaders as an advocate for volunteers.

☐ Clarify the roles and interrelationships of the volunteer department with the public relations staff, personnel or human resources department, the development office, staff responsible for special events, and any other unit with responsibilities related to involvement of volunteers.

13. Volunteer Input

Too many organizations want help, not input. Volunteers bring a different perspective from employees or clients. This point of view may result from being less vested in the professional process, or from being younger or older, or from simply having the distance that a part-time schedule allows. Volunteers are in a position to observe the organization and can take more risks in criticizing or speaking out. Develop ways to let their perspective be heard or volunteers will either cause friction or leave. Also, actively seek practical and innovative ideas from volunteers.

EXECUTIVE ROLE:

☐ Develop channels for allowing volunteers to voice ideas and suggestions, including criticisms.

☐ Be open to considering volunteers' ideas. Respond to such ideas, even if you must explain why the suggestion cannot be implemented.

☐ Utilize volunteers to form collaborations between your organization and other community groups, especially if there are obstacles such as formal areas of jurisdiction.

☐ Maximize the special/unique benefits of volunteers on a day-to-day basis: use volunteers as a sounding board and ask them to give you honest reactions to plans; tap their knowledge of the community.

☐ Schedule time for members of administration to meet volunteers individually and in small groups as a "think tank." (By the way, this is a very meaningful form of recognition.)

☐ Be accessible to meeting with volunteers personally when appropriate.

☐ Make sure that any agency program evaluation includes the surveying of volunteers.

☐ Be sure that volunteers are tapped to serve on agency planning committees, advisory groups and board sub-committees.

14. Volunteers as Supporters

Volunteers are a powerful corps of supporters if you make use of their perspectives and influence, but volunteers do not become effective advocates for your organization spontaneously. In order for volunteers to be the best public relations agents, they need accurate information. On a regular basis, keep volunteers informed about new services, changes in personnel, and issues impacting your agency. Find specific ways for volunteers to become external messengers about your work.

EXECUTIVE ROLE:

☐ Give each volunteer three agency brochures and ask him/her to give them to people who might benefit from knowing about your services.

☐ Ask volunteers to write to funders, legislators, or the newspaper about what they have learned about your agency/cause while doing volunteer work with you.

☐ Select a work project that requires lots of hands and ask each volunteer to bring one friend or relative for three hours to help accomplish the task. The project is an end unto itself, will make all who participate feel good, and does more to publicize your usefulness to the community than speeches do.

☐ Consider whether periodic meetings to inform volunteers about your plans for the future might not yield positive results.

☐ Add volunteers to your newsletter mailing list or even to in-house memo distribution, to increase their ability to speak accurately on your behalf.

Underlying everything in the checklist above is your role in setting the tone for volunteer involvement. Your personal support and enthusiasm (or lack of it) will be obvious to volunteers and employees alike. Your willingness to allocate organization resources and time on your own schedule for volunteers validates that community participants are indeed part of the personnel team.

A Last Word about Your Role

You also provide leadership in making volunteer involvement integral to the work of your organization. You can put the subject of volunteers "on the agenda," finding opportunities to ask "are we doing the best job of tapping volunteer skills in this area?" Including the director of volunteers and, when appropriate, representative volunteers themselves, on such committees as quality assurance or long-range planning sends a message to everyone—and gives you valuable input.

There is something else to say about recognition, too. We sometimes confuse "recognition" with "appreciation." These are not the same thing and do not always go together. Their common denominator is "acknowledgment." Perhaps the sincerest form of recognition is to see one's ideas put into action. Both employees and volunteers want to see that they make a difference. The annual volunteer recognition event is not an end, it's a beginning to the next year. Volunteers—and paid staff—should leave re-motivated and recommitted. As executive, this is also your opportunity to articulate and reaffirm your vision for the potential of volunteer involvement.

CONCLUSION

Historically, volunteers were the pioneers, the innovators who recognized existing community needs and found ways to meet them. Almost every institution and profession we take for granted today owes its initial establishment to the efforts of citizens who chose to become involved in a cause. Such pioneering continues to be a part of the volunteer picture today. In 1986, I noted that the previous decade had seen volunteers institute hospice programs, services to victims of abuse, and projects looking ahead to space colonization—just to name a few. In the ten years since, volunteers have been instrumental in founding innumerable services to people with AIDS, programs to help "crack babies," and previously inconceivable forms of virtual interaction on the Internet. The organization you head may well be able to name the key volunteers who filed your incorporation papers and made up your first board. Some of them may even still be around to see the fruits of their early labor.

The media in the 80's gravitated towards labels such as "the me generation" or "self-involved Yuppies." Today's dismay is over the negativity of "Generation X" or the disillusionment of the middle class. Volunteering is the antithesis of such negative images. All the studies and polls prove that the vast majority of Americans do become involved in their communities. In fact, volunteering is so pervasive, we tend to take it for granted. And, as discussed throughout this book, there are many exciting new sources of people seeking ways to serve, whatever vocabulary they may use to identify themselves. Volunteerism has truly become "community resource mobilization."

Legislative and economic changes continue to create uncertainty about the future of many nonprofit organizations and government services. Volunteering has been tossed into the limelight, often for the wrong reasons. The question is not whether volunteers can fill budget gaps, but whether organizations are truly prepared to utilize volunteers in teamwork with paid staff.

Peter Drucker, one of the top management experts today, tells business leaders that "your people are your greatest asset," an assertion equally if not more true in nonprofit and government agencies. The most effective executives in the future will learn to lead, not manage, to bring out the best in employees and volunteers. "People raising" comes before fund raising.

From the Top Down presents executives with the challenge of tapping community resources to the maximum. Volunteers cannot fully and successfully contribute to an organization unless they receive visibility and management attention. You have the authority and power necessary to set the tone for volunteer involvement in your organization—your vision and commitment will provide leadership for paid and volunteer staff alike.

APPENDIX

VOLUNTEER MANAGEMENT TASK OUTLINE

The following is an outline of the major functions and responsibilities necessary to the effective management of a volunteer program. These are the main headings excerpted from a much more detailed "Volunteer Management Task Analysis" published in Chapter 3 of *The (Help!) I-Don't-Have-Enough-Time Guide to Volunteer Management* by Katherine Noyes Campbell and Susan J. Ellis (Energize, 1995). This outline provides you with a sense of the scope of the job of directing volunteers. Use it as a starting point from which to write a job description for the position of leader of volunteers in your organization.

I. PROGRAM PLANNING AND ADMINISTRATION

    A. Assess/analyze agency and client needs for assistance.

    B. Articulate a vision for volunteer involvement in the organization.

    C. Develop volunteer program goals and objectives.

    D. Design volunteer assignments.

    E. Develop risk management procedures and strategies.

    F. Coordinate schedules.

    G. Set policies and procedures.

H. Manage budget.

I. Meet space, supply and other support needs.

J. Advocate for volunteers.

K. Develop new projects.

L. Develop own professional skills.

II. RECRUITMENT AND PUBLIC RELATIONS

A. Plan recruitment strategies.

B. Develop recruitment and media relations materials.

C. Handle public speaking and personal contacts.

D. Manage ongoing recruitment efforts.

III. INTERVIEWING AND SCREENING

A. Prepare for applicants.

B. Conduct interviews.

C. Screen candidates.

D. Assign volunteers.

E. Facilitate group volunteer involvement.

IV. ORIENTATION AND TRAINING

A. Develop an orientation program for all volunteers, regardless of assignment.

B. Offer staff development in how to work effectively with volunteers.

C. Design initial training plan.

D. Develop in-service training options.

E. Prepare manuals and handbooks.

V. SUPERVISION

A. Handle direct supervision of volunteers and employees working with the volunteer office.

B. Handle indirect supervision, supporting those to whom volunteers are assigned.

C. Be a liaison, available to all volunteers and salaried staff as next step in the "chain of command."

D. Manage individual volunteer performance assessment.

VI. MOTIVATION AND RECOGNITION

A. Assure ongoing volunteer motivation and appreciation.

B. Plan and conduct recognition activities.

C. Develop "career ladders" for volunteers.

VII. PROGRAM EVALUATION

A. Conduct regular program evaluation.

B. Assess ongoing progress in all program components.

VIII. RECORDKEEPING AND REPORTING

A. Develop a comprehensive volunteer recordkeeping system.

B. Maintain system.

C. Develop reports.

IX. OTHER RESPONSIBILITIES

A. Participate in agency fundraising events, coordinating volunteer assistance.

B. Solicit in-kind donations to assist agency services.

C. Represent the organization at community functions; represent the organization to visiting community members.

D. Provide technical assistance to other agency volunteer efforts, such as board development, working with auxiliaries, etc.

E. Promote volunteerism as an avenue for personal and professional growth, and as a resource for addressing community problems.

APPENDIX

VOLUNTEERISM RESOURCES

Volunteerism is growing as a distinct management discipline and volunteer administration is emerging as a profession. This means that the skills of developing and managing volunteers are being codified so that newcomers to this responsibility can learn from the experience of their predecessors.

It should be noted that "volunteerism" is a different discipline than "voluntarism," despite the fact that these two words are often confused. Voluntarism refers to all voluntary activities in a society (in the United States that includes religion, for example) and covers issues of concern to voluntary, not-for-profit agencies. Volunteerism, on the other hand, refers to anything involving volunteers and volunteering, regardless of setting. Government agencies, which are not part of the "voluntary sector," may indeed be included under the umbrella of "volunteerism" when it comes to volunteers active in courts, parks and recreation, and all other such public services.

In most geographic areas it is increasingly possible to obtain some training in volunteer administration, either through a formal academic institution or through workshops sponsored by a wide array of organizations. Books and journals on volunteerism are available. Conferences for leaders of volunteer programs have also proliferated on both the state and national levels.

As executive, you should expect your director of volunteers to become familiar with such resources and to become active in relevant professional associations. It is important to encourage the director of volunteers to seek out colleagues in volunteerism generically, as well as those in settings similar to yours. Many of the approaches and techniques successfully utilized in other types of organizations can be applied with equal success in any setting.

If you do not already have a director of volunteers, you may need to become familiar with volunteerism resources yourself, or help the staff member you have designated to work with volunteers as a part-time responsibility to make use of such resources. Leadership-level volunteers themselves may also benefit from such training and information.

Here are some of the most commonly-available places in which to seek information on volunteerism.

Volunteer Centers   Volunteer Centers, also called Voluntary Action Centers or Volunteer Bureaus in some cities, are local clearinghouses for information on volunteer opportunities. Organizations seeking volunteers can "register" their needs, while members of the public can contact the Volunteer Center to discover what volunteer assignments are available.

Different Volunteer Centers engage in different projects. Some publish a directory of local volunteer opportunities while others actually interview potential volunteers and try to individualize the assistance in finding the right volunteer job. Many Centers organize community-wide events for National Volunteer Week (occurring annually in April) or coordinate collaborative recruitment efforts such as shopping mall fairs. The larger Volunteer Centers also maintain libraries of materials on volunteer program development.

If your community has a Volunteer Center, by all means get on its mailing list. This should assure you of receiving information about local training workshops, conferences, or meetings focused on volunteerism.

Because Volunteer Centers are nonprofit institutions (many are funded through United Way), the majority of their services are offered free of charge or at low cost. It may even be possible to receive consultation from them in how to start your volunteer program or in how to locate a director of volunteers.

Whether or not your community   **DOVIAs and**
has a Volunteer Center, it may have   **State Associations**
what come to be called, generical-
ly, a "DOVIA." This stands for
"Directors of Volunteers in Agencies" and is simply an association
of people who have the responsibility for leading the volunteer
program in their organizations. DOVIAs usually meet on a regular basis several times a year and operate as self-help professional groups. They plan their meetings to provide a mixture of col-
legial interaction (often the main benefit of attending) and provision of information. There is usually a speaker who addresses
the group about some aspect of volunteer management.

The more established DOVIAs sponsor periodic workshops
at which nationally-known trainers may be invited to present.
Newsletters and other forms of resource exchange are also common. All costs for these activities are covered through membership dues or registration fees. Often the Volunteer Center offers
some staff support for the local DOVIA.

Your state or province may also have an active statewide
association for volunteerism, bringing together leaders of volunteer efforts for conferences and legislative advocacy.

More than half the states have a   **State Offices and**
state-level   government   office   **Commissions**
charged with coordinating volun-
teerism. Such offices have names
that are some version of State Office on Voluntary Citizen
Participation, Governor's Office on Volunteerism, etc. Their man-
dates range as widely as their names, but all attempt to be
statewide clearinghouses of information about citizen involvement. In some ways, State Offices function as Volunteer Centers
for a wider geographic area.

Again, be sure you are on the mailing list of your State
Office, if you are lucky enough to be in a state that has one. The
good State Offices sponsor statewide conferences for volunteer
leaders and publish informational newsletters.

As a result of 1993 Federal legislation, most states estab-
lished Governor-appointed "Commissions on Community
Service" to administer programs funded by the Corporation for
National and Community Service. In some states, these commis-

sions are staffed by and work very closely with the existing State Offices of Volunteerism. In other states, the commissions operate as separate entities.

National and   On the national (and increasingly
International   on the international) level there
Resources   are several organizations devoted
                                to furthering volunteerism general-
ly, as well as some focused on one or another specific field of volunteer activity.

• The three major generic organizations and their quarterly publications are:

Association for Volunteer Administration (AVA), P.O. Box 4584, Boulder, CO 80306. 303-541-0238
    —Publishes *The Journal of Volunteer Administration*
    —Runs a professional certification program and produces a *Statement of Professional Ethics*
    —Sponsors an annual International Conference on Volunteer Administration in October

Points of Light Foundation, 1737 H Street, NW, Washington, DC 20006. 202-223-9186
    —Publishes *Volunteer Leadership*
    —Runs the Council on Workplace Volunteerism and the National Council of Volunteer Centers
    —Holds an annual National Community Service Conference in June
    —Produces "Volunteer Community Service Catalog" with books and recognition items
    —Sponsors National Volunteer Week (April) and coordinates the President's Volunteer Service Awards

Association for Research on Nonprofit Organizations and Voluntary Action (ARNOVA), c/o Indiana University Center on Philanthropy, 550 West North Street, Suite 301, Indianapolis, IN 46202-3162.
    —Publishes *Nonprofit and Voluntary Sector Quarterly*
    —Holds an annual conference in the fall

• The Federal agency in the United States responsible for issues relating to community service and volunteering is:

Corporation for National and Community Service, 1100 Vermont Avenue, NW, Washington, DC 20525. 202-606-5000
—Includes AmeriCorps, Learn & Serve America, VISTA and other programs; National Senior Service Corps programs under the agency when it was called ACTION, such as Retired and Senior Volunteer Program (RSVP), Foster Grandparents, and Senior Companion programs

• Other national or international organizations with more specialized interests are:

American Association for Museum Volunteers (AAMV), 1225 Eye Street, NW, Washington, DC 20005. 202-289-6575

American Society for Directors of Volunteer Services (ASDVS) of the American Hospital Association, 840 North Lake Shore Drive, Chicago, IL 60611.

Canadian Centre for Philanthropy, 1329 Bay Street, Toronto, ON M5R 2C4. 416-515-0764

City Cares of America, 1737 H Street, NW, Washington, DC 20006. 202-887-0500 (Organizes group volunteer projects for busy professionals in a number of major cities.)

Independent Sector, 1828 L Street, NW, Washington, DC 20026. 202-223-8100 (Among other advocacy interests, conducts research about giving and volunteering.)

International Association for Justice Volunteerism (IAJV), P. O. Box 7172, Pueblo West, CO 81007. 719-547-4204

National Association of Community Leadership Organizations (NACLO), 525 W. Meridian St., Suite 102, Indianapolis, IN 46225. 317-637-7408

National Association of Partners in Education (NAPE), 209
   Madison St., Suite 401, Alexandria, VA 22314. 703-836-4880

National Center for Nonprofit Boards, Suite 510-S, 2000 L Street,
   NW, Washington, DC 20036. 202-452-6262

Youth Service America, 1101 15th St., NW, Suite 200, Washington,
   DC 20005. 202-296-2992

   Because of the changing nature of the field, any published
list of resources will be in need of some correction or update
almost as soon as it is put on the printed page. When you are
ready to seek out the organizations just described, start by connecting with your local resources such as the Volunteer Center—
or contact a director of volunteers in any major community
agency.

Insurance Resources   Also a fluid category, there is at
                             least one insurance program devel-
                             oped to cover the unique needs of
                             a volunteer project by providing
excess accident and liability insurance: Volunteers Insurance
Service, 216 S. Peyton Street, Alexandria, VA 22314, 800-468-
4200.
   The Nonprofit Risk Management Center, 1001 Connecticut
Ave., NW, Suite 900, Washington, DC 20036, 202-785-3891, has
produced pioneering books on volunteer risk-related subjects.
Several were mentioned in Chapter 9 and are listed in the bibliography that follows. The Center also publishes a newsletter and
answers technical assistance questions.

BIBLIOGRAPHY

   During the past decade there has been a steady increase in
the number of publications related to volunteer management.
While the following list is by no means intended to be all-inclu-
sive, or even comprehensive, it is a starting point for those learning more about the principles and practices of volunteer management.

Readers may also want to contact Energize, Inc. for our annual "Volunteer Energy Resource Catalog" of more than fifty-five books, videos, software and other resources (* following a reference denotes those books available from Energize). You can find us at 5450 Wissahickon Avenue, Philadelphia, PA   19144, 1-800-395-9800.

Brudney, Jeffrey. *Fostering Volunteer Programs in the Public Sector*. San Francisco: Jossey-Bass, 1990.*

Campbell, Katherine Noyes and Susan J. Ellis. *The (Help!) I-Don't-Have-Enough-Time Guide to Volunteer Management*. Philadelphia: Energize, Inc., 1995.*

Connors, Tracy Daniel, ed. *The Volunteer Management Handbook*. New York: John Wiley & Sons, 1995.

Ellis, Susan J. *The Board's Role in Volunteer Involvement*. Washington, DC: National Center for Nonprofit Boards, 1995.*

Ellis, Susan J. *The Volunteer Management Audit*. Alexandria, VA: United Way of America, 1992.*

Ellis, Susan J. *The Volunteer Recruitment Book*. Philadelphia: Energize, Inc., 1994.*

Ellis, Susan J. and Katherine H. Noyes. *Proof Positive: Developing Significant Volunteer Recordkeeping Systems*, revised ed. Philadelphia: Energize, Inc., 1990.*

Fisher, James C. and Kathleen M. Cole. *Leadership and Management of Volunteer Programs: A Guide for Volunteer Administrators*. San Francisco: Jossey-Bass, 1993.*

Graff, Linda. *By Definition: Policies for Volunteer Programs*. Toronto: Volunteer Ontario, 1993.*

Karn, G. Neil. "The True Dollar Value of Volunteers," Parts I and II, *The Journal of Volunteer Administration*. Vol. I, Nos. 2 and 3, 1982.

McCurley, Steve and Rick Lynch. *Essentials of Volunteer Management.* Downers Grove, IL: Heritage Arts Publishing, 1989.

Patterson, John with Charles Tremper and Pam Rypkema. *Child Abuse Prevention Primer for Your Organization.* Washington, DC: Nonprofit Risk Management Center, 1995.*

Patterson, John with Charles Tremper and Pam Rypkema. *Staff Screening Tool Kit: Keeping Bad Apples Out of Your Organization.* Washington, DC: Nonprofit Risk Management Center, 1994.*

Points of Light Foundation. *Changing the Paradigm.* Report and materials from the Changing the Paradigm project initiated in 1991 to determine the characteristics of highly-effective volunteer programs, including several report booklets and a Self-Assessment Kit. Washington, DC: 1992-1995.

Scheier, Ivan H. *Building Staff/Volunteer Relations.* Philadelphia: Energize, Inc., 1993*

Tremper, Charles and Gwynne Kostin. *No Surprises: Controlling Risks in Volunteer Programs.* Washington, DC: Nonprofit Risk Management Center, 1993.*

Vineyard, Sue and Stephen McCurley, eds. *Managing Volunteer Diversity: A Rainbow of Opportunities.* Downers Grove, IL: Heritage Arts Publishing, 1992.

Wroblewski, Celeste J. *The Seven Rs of Volunteer Development: A YMCA Resource Kit.* Chicago: YMCA of the USA, 1994.*

Other Resources

For information on computerizing volunteer records, contact Energize for a demo disk of the *Volunteer Information Management (V.I.M.)* software from BWB Associates, Ltd.

Energize has produced a videotape entitled "Colleagues: The Volunteer/Employee Relationship," designed for use in training sessions for frontline staff who work with volunteers. Call for price and preview details.

INDEX

ABOUT THE AUTHOR

Susan J. Ellis is President of Energize, Inc., a training, consulting, and publishing firm that specializes in volunteerism. She founded the Philadelphia-based company in 1977 based on her experiences in developing and running volunteer programs in justice and cultural arts settings. She has since assisted a wide range of clients in almost every state, four Canadian provinces, and South America to create or strengthen their volunteer corps. Since 1992, she has expanded her work to Europe. At least once a year she travels across the Atlantic to speak at Volonteurope conferences, work with clients in Scandinavia, or conduct training seminars across the United Kingdom.

Susan is the author or co-author of nine books, including *By the People: A History of Americans as Volunteers* and *The Volunteer Recruitment Book.* Since 1990, she has been the national columnist "On Volunteers" for *The NonProfit Times.* From 1981 to 1987, Susan was editor-in-chief of *The Journal of Volunteer Administration* and still serves as its manuscripts developer. She has written more than eighty articles for publications as varied as *The Chronicle of Philanthropy* and *Credit Union Magazine.*

In 1995, Energize became the Forum Manager for the "Volunteer Central" area of the access.point Civic Involvement System on America Online. Susan's interest in interactive computer technology is also expressed as an advisory committee member of Impact Online, a nonprofit dedicated to increasing the community service value of cyberspace and virtual volunteering.

She was the recipient of the Association for Volunteer Administration's 1989 Harriet Naylor Distinguished Member Service Award. Susan is active in a variety of local, state and national volunteerism associations.